D0445885

PARIS
Quiz

PARIS
Quiz

HOW WELL DO YOU KNOW PARIS?

Dominique Lesbros

THE LITTLE BOOKROOM • NEW YORK

© 2009 The Little Bookroom

Book Design: Sarah Caplan, MPH Design
Translation: Andrew Branch

Originally published as Paris Quiz
© 2007 éditions Parigramme /
Compagnie parisienne du livre (Paris)

Library of Congress Cataloging-in-Publication Data

Lesbros, Dominique. [Paris quiz. English]
Paris quiz / by Dominique Lesbros ; translated by Andrew Branch.
p. cm.
Originally published in French. Paris : Parigramme, 2007.
ISBN 978-1-892145-82-6 (alk. paper)
1. Paris (France)—Miscellanea. I. Title.
DC707.L474413 2009
944'.361–dc22   2009011569

Published by The Little Bookroom
435 Hudson Street, 3rd Floor, New York, NY 10014
editorial@littlebookroom.com
www.littlebookroom.com

All rights reserved, which includes the right to
reproduce this book or portions thereof
in any form whatsoever.

2 4 6 8 0 9 7 5 3

*Merci à Florence, Isabelle, Hélène et Caroline, mes voisines
d'eau douce, d'avoir bien voulu travailler des méninges
pour me fournir de vraies fausses réponses.*

Contents

Introduction

Let's forget for a moment the workaday Paris, and look at the capital in a new light.

What if Paris were nothing but a giant playing field? What if the roads, the monuments, the statues and the history of the capital were the pretext for a thousand questions?

The questions that follow are each provided with three possible answers, one true —the other two far-fetched, deceptive, treacherous at times.

But be careful! In exceptional cases, more than one answer may be correct. Will you be able to recognize them?

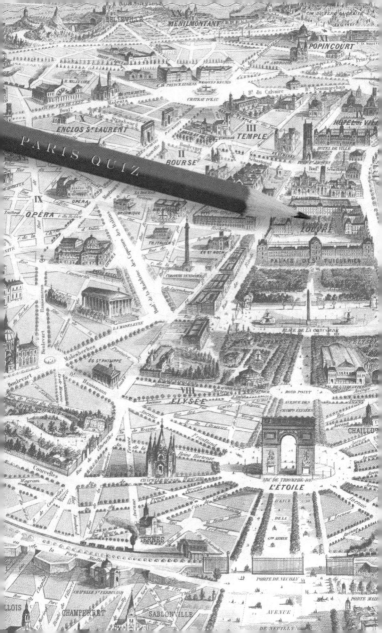

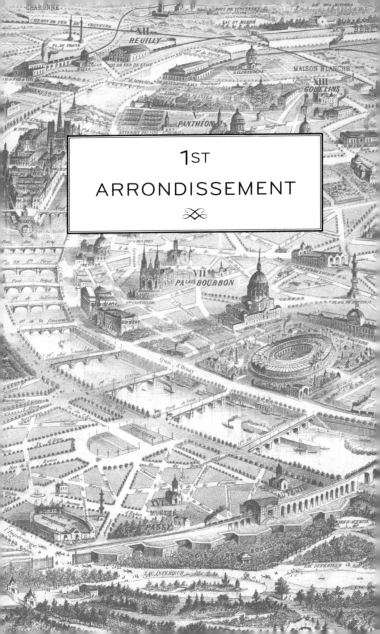

1ST
ARRONDISSEMENT

1. **Why did the engineer Baltard carry out the construction of the pavilions at Les Halles, assigned to him by Napoleon III, extremely reluctantly?**

   ☐ a. He was very poorly compensated
   ☐ b. He hated iron
   ☐ c. He disapproved of the chosen site

2. **What do the bas-reliefs on the Vendôme column depict?**

   ☐ a. The Austrian campaign
   ☐ b. The Egyptian campaign
   ☐ c. The Italian campaign

3. **What site inspired the abbot Delille, in the 18th century, to write the following verses?**

   In this garden everything is encountered,
   Except the shade of flowers,
   If one upsets one's morals there,
   At least one sets one's watch

   ☐ a. The Tuileries gardens
   ☐ b. The Carrousel gardens
   ☐ c. The Palais-Royal gardens

4. **During the Franco-Prussian war a Prussian officer came to the café Le Véry, situated on the edge of the Palais-Royal garden, and asked that he be given a cup "from which no Frenchman had ever drunk." What vessel was his drink served in?**

   ☐ a. A chamber pot
   ☐ b. An old boot
   ☐ c. A rusty moneybox

5. Under the archways of the Palais-Royal are dozens of shops, as curious as they are old-fashioned, displaying in their windows oriental pipes, lead soldiers and music boxes. One even specializes in medals and other decorations. Is the free sale of these awards permitted?

   ☐ a. No, their sale is subject to strict regulation
   ☐ b. Yes, but only on the presentation of evidence of the award or a declaration on one's honor
   ☐ c. Yes, anyone can buy one without precondition

6. According to legend, the Tuileries were long haunted by a strange character, the "little red man of the Tuileries" who, like the "white woman" of the Hapsburgs, appeared to kings as a morbid warning. What did he signal?

   ☐ a. Their impending death
   ☐ b. A great epidemic
   ☐ c. An imminent war

7. On the north face of the Carrousel's Arc de Triomphe (facing the Tuileries garden), a statue by Dumont depicts a "sapeur." The portrait is of a soldier in the Grande Armée, whose name lives on in a popular expression. Which?

   ☐ a. To do a Mariolle
   ☐ b. To do a Zouave
   ☐ c. To live a Patachon life

8. **What shape is the Tuileries pool closest to the place de la Concorde?**

   ☐ a. Round
   ☐ b. Square
   ☐ c. Octagonal

9. **What became of the fontaine des Innocents, upon the great restoration of Les Halles during the 1970s?**

   ☐ a. It was relocated to the place de l'Hotel-de-Ville
   ☐ b. It was perched on a metal scaffold
   ☐ c. It was simply taken apart, stone by stone

10. **What picturesque characters, famous for their large-brimmed hats, traditionally offer a bouquet of lilies to the President of the Republic on the 1st of May?**

    ☐ a. The Savoyards de Drouot (the Savoyards of the Drouot auction house)
    ☐ b. The "forts des Halles" (strongmen of Les Halles)
    ☐ c. The "bougnats Auvergnats" (Coalmen of Auvergne)

11. **What goods were exchanged in pavilion no. 8 of the old Forum des Halles, which was saved from demolition and set up at Nogent-sur-Marne?**

    ☐ a. Fruits and vegetables
    ☐ b. Eggs and fowl
    ☐ c. Offal

12. At what address on the quai des Orfèvres is the headquarters of the judicial police, nicknamed the "French Chicken House Corporation," located?

   ☐ a. At no. 14
   ☐ b. At no. 22
   ☐ c. At no. 36

13. The maison Bosc, situated on the Île de la Cité, has made official outfits to cut and color standards personally set down by Napoleon I since 1845. For whom are the costumes made?

   ☐ a. Diplomats
   ☐ b. Members of the bar
   ☐ c. Soldiers

14. Why is one of the towers of the Conciergerie called "la tour Bonbec" ("Good Beak Tower")?

   ☐ a. It was where torturers loosened prisoners' tongues
   ☐ b. The kitchens were located in it
   ☐ c. It's shaped like a bird's beak

15. What décor adorns the ceilings of Sainte-Chapelle?

   ☐ a. A midnight blue sky sprinkled with golden stars
   ☐ b. A fresco showing God on a cloud, surrounded by angels flying through a clear sky
   ☐ c. Scenes from the life of Christ

16. **What is the courtyard of the principal entrance to the Palais de Justice called?**

☐ a. La cour d'Amené
☐ b. La cour de Mai
☐ c. La cour Desmets

17. **What is unique about the rue de Viarmes?**

☐ a. It is the only circular road in Paris
☐ b. There are no house numbers on the fronts of the houses along it
☐ c. It is the oldest paved road in Paris

18. **Where does the name of the old La Samaritaine shops come from?**

☐ a. From a 17th century fountain, today demolished
☐ b. From a crinoline dress considered very stylish in the 18th century
☐ c. From a vaudeville theatre that served as a tobacconist at the end of the 19th century

19. **Under Louis-Philippe the place de la Concorde was decorated with statues of women symbolizing the great cities of France, placed on the perimeter of the square according to the actual geographic position of the cities. Why did the Toulousains complain about this arrangement?**

☐ a. The statue representing Toulouse is repulsively ugly
☐ b. Toulouse's representative was placed, by accident, at the north of the square
☐ c. The "pink city" was simply left out

20. **How long did it take to transport the obelisk presented to France by Egypt in 1830?**

    ☐ a. Five and a half months
    ☐ b. One year, one month and one day
    ☐ c. Two years and 24 days

21. **How does the form of the glass pyramid at the Louvre compare to that of the great pyramid of Giza?**

    ☐ a. They have roughly the same dimensions
    ☐ b. The Giza pyramid is ten times larger
    ☐ c. The Louvre pyramid is much more pointed

22. **What is unique about the Saint-Germain-l'Auxerrois church?**

    ☐ a. There is, at regular hours, a concert of its bells
    ☐ b. It's the only church that celebrates marriages during the week
    ☐ c. The nave isn't facing Jerusalem

23. **For what figure on the brink of death did the priests of the parish of Saint-Eustache refuse to rouse themselves on the evening of February 17, 1673?**

    ☐ a. Ninon de Lenclos
    ☐ b. Voltaire
    ☐ c. Molière

24. **Where does the name of the Pyramides metro station come from?**

   ☐ a. From the shape of the square situated above-ground
   ☐ b. From a Napoleonic victory in Egypt
   ☐ c. From the glass pyramid at the Louvre, right next to the station

25. **Under what name did the modern musée du Louvre open its doors to the public, on the 10th of August 1793?**

   ☐ a. The Free Citizens' Museum
   ☐ b. The Grand Gallery of Fine Arts
   ☐ c. The Central Museum of Art

26. **The place du Châtelet occupies the site of the old Grand Châtelet, a sinister edifice that served as a court and prison during the Middle Ages. A system of expedited justice pronounced sentence according to the crime committed: killers were hanged, heretics burned...what became of counterfeiters?**

   ☐ a. They were scalded
   ☐ b. They were stoned
   ☐ c. They were quartered

27. **What profession were Messieurs Véro and Dodat practicing when they first opened the covered arcade that bears their names?**

   ☐ a. They had made a fortune as jewelers
   ☐ b. They ran a theatre
   ☐ c. They were butchers

28. **Sainte-Chapelle was constructed in 1246 to house what relics?**

    ☐ a. The crown of thorns and a fragment of the cross
    ☐ b. One of St. Luke's fingers and three beard hairs from St. Peter
    ☐ c. The holy shroud and a cup that Jesus drank from

29. **In the waiting room of the Palais de Justice, a monument dedicated to the great orator Berryer is flanked by two statues of seated women. The woman on the right symbolizes the law and rests her left foot on an animal. What kind?**

    ☐ a. A snail
    ☐ b. A tortoise
    ☐ c. A snake

30. **Under the reign of what monarch was the Louvre started in 1190?**

    ☐ a. Philippe Auguste
    ☐ b. Philippe le Bel
    ☐ c. Saint Louis

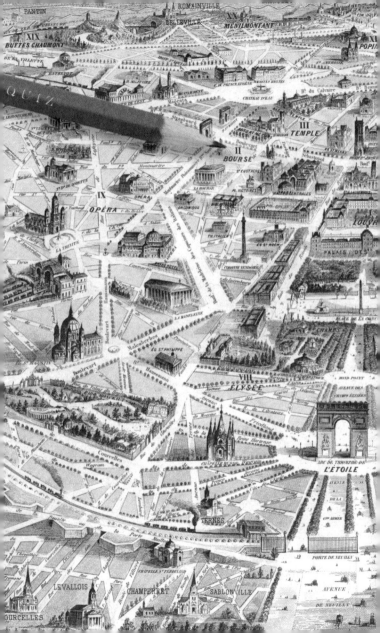

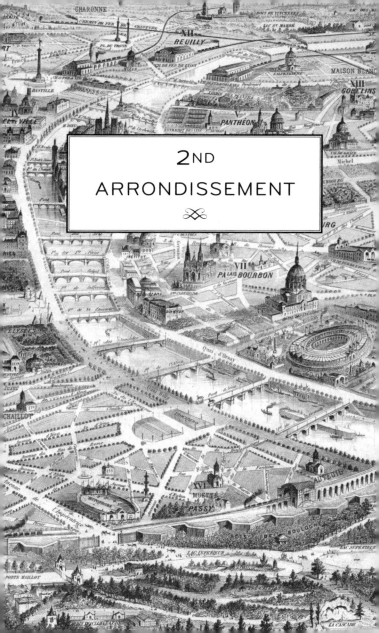

2ND
ARRONDISSEMENT

⚜

1. **A bronze equestrian statue of Louis XIV occupies the center of the place des Victoires. What position is the horse in?**

   ☐ a. Its four hoofs are on the ground
   ☐ b. It's rearing up on its back limbs
   ☐ c. It's bucking, its front limbs to the ground

2. **Every trade has a patron saint, sometimes due to the most curious associations: St. Laurent — burned alive as a martyr — is the patron saint of rotisserie operators. What profession is under the protection of "Our Lady of Good News"?**

   ☐ a. Radio and television workers
   ☐ b. Notaries and executors of wills
   ☐ c. Mailmen and postal workers

3. **What good news did the habitants of the Bonne-Nouvelle quarter celebrate in 1667?**

   ☐ a. A royal birth
   ☐ b. The cleaning up of the cour des Miracles by police forces
   ☐ c. The elimination of a tax

4. **The place du Caire is located on the site of the old cour des Miracles (the court of miracles). Where does the name of this famous court come from?**

   ☐ a. St. Louis performed miraculous healings at the spot
   ☐ b. Small shows called "miracles" were performed there for passersby
   ☐ c. It was a meeting place of beggars who faked being maimed

5. **What animal was at the heart of one of the greatest coups in financial history?**

   ☐ a. A carrier pigeon
   ☐ b. A police dog
   ☐ c. The parakeet of the banker Law

6. **What is unique about the rue de Degrés?**

   ☐ a. There are no doorways along its sides
   ☐ b. It's the shortest in Paris
   ☐ c. It's in the form of stairs

7. **What incident marred the unfolding of jury deliberations for 1983's prix Goncourt at the restaurant Drouant?**

   ☐ a. The president of the jury had a pie thrown in his face
   ☐ b. Microphones were found hidden under the table
   ☐ c. Powerful sleeping medicine had been put in the dessert wine

8. **The name of Jean sans Peur (the fearless) can't be taken too literally; he was only able to calm his fright by constructing, around the year 1410, a fortified tower that can be seen on the rue Étienne-Marcel. What exactly was he afraid of?**

   ☐ a. Popular riots
   ☐ b. Retaliation
   ☐ c. Catching the plague

9. **What theatre did Offenbach found in 1855?**

   ☐ a. The théâtre de la Michodière
   ☐ b. The Opéra-Comique
   ☐ c. The théâtre des Bouffes-Parisiens

10. **What picturesque name did the rue Dussoubs bear in the 13th century?**

    ☐ a. La rue du Dessous-de-Bras (underarm road)
    ☐ b. La rue Sens-Dessus-Dessous (upside-down road)
    ☐ c. La rue Gratte-Cul (scratch-bottom road)

11. **Why did the statue of General Desaix cause a scandal upon its erection in the place des Victoires in 1810?**

    ☐ a. Because it showed a naked man
    ☐ b. Because the man's name was considered licentious in and of itself
    ☐ c. Because Desaix was a notorious libertine

12. **During the 17th century, the cour des Miracles was a hideout for crooks who made themselves up as maimed beggars to gain the pity of passersby and squeeze a few coins from them. What did they do to simulate streaks of spittle on their faces?**

    ☐ a. They ate bits of soap
    ☐ b. They let dogs lick their faces
    ☐ c. They let snails run across their chins

13. **What is the real name of the old stock exchange?**

    ☐ a. The Palais Brogniart
    ☐ b. The Palais Brongniart
    ☐ c. The Palais Grogniard

14. **What is the longest covered arcade in the capital?**

    ☐ a. The passage des Panoramas
    ☐ b. The passage du Grand-Cer
    ☐ c. The passage du Caire

15. **At no. 13 galerie Vivienne lived Vidocq, who was…**

    ☐ a. A detective in the service of the emperor
    ☐ b. A convict who became the chief of police
    ☐ c. A policeman who became a gentleman bandit, head of a band of policemen robbers

16. **What writer, who grew up living on the passage Choiseul, remembers in one of his novels: "you have to admit that the Passage is an unbelievable cesspit"?**

    ☐ a. Jean Genet
    ☐ b. Louis-Ferdinand Céline
    ☐ c. Albert Camus

17. **One side of the place du Caire is distinguished by Egyptian-campaign-inspired decoration. In it, one can identify hieroglyphics and the face of a goddess. Which?**

    ☐ a. Hathor
    ☐ b. Bastet
    ☐ c. Serket

18. **A sculpture representing an angel stands against the apartment building at 57 rue du Turbigo. What's unique about this statue compared to others in Paris?**

    ☐ a. It's the biggest
    ☐ b. It's the only lone caryatid
    ☐ c. It's the only one that is completely naked

19. What type of building, located at 32 rue Blondel, is included on the list of national historic monuments?

☐ a. A house of ill repute
☐ b. A public bath
☐ c. A public toilet from the beginning of the 19th century

20. What equipment was the avenue de l'Opéra the first to have in 1878?

☐ a. Crosswalks
☐ b. Electric streetlights
☐ c. Public benches

21. The rue Lulli pays homage to the famous court ballet composer and director of the Académie royal de musique, who met an uncommon end. Of what did he die, on the 22nd of March 1687?

☐ a. He choked on an olive
☐ b. He bumped into a beam
☐ c. He drove his conductor's baton into his foot

22. What galerie was converted to compete with the galerie Vivienne around 1826?

☐ a. The galerie du Palais-Royal
☐ b. The galerie Colbert
☐ c. The galerie Véro-Dodat

23. What historic event does the name of the Quatre-Septembre street and metro station refer to?

☐ a. The adoption of the tricolor flag in 1790
☐ b. The proclamation of the third republic in 1870
☐ c. The legislative vote ensuring the right to retirement in 1910

24. Maison Stern, until recently in business in the passage des Panoramas since 1834, is the official supplier of what product to every royal court in Europe?

☐ a. Hats and canes
☐ b. Business cards
☐ c. Diadems and crowns

25. In the 19th century, panoramas were vast circular trompe-l'oeil paintings, made to be viewed from the center of a rotunda. What did these paintings depict?

☐ a. Views of Paris and of great foreign cities
☐ b. Battle scenes
☐ c. Episodes from the life of Christ

26. What man of letters directed *La Dame de chez Maxim*, about a provincial man tasting the gallant charms of Paris?

☐ a. Georges Feydeau
☐ b. Eugène Labiche
☐ c. Georges Courteline

27. The croque-monsieur, a dish on the menu of every Parisian brasserie, was born in the 2nd arrondissement. True or false?

☐ a. True
☐ b. False

28. What happened to Stendahl on the 22nd of March 1842, on the sidewalk of the boulevard des Capucines?

☐ a. He ran into the actress Mélanie Gulbert and fell in love with her
☐ b. Inspired by the animated boulevard, he came up with the framework for his novel *Le Rouge et le Noir*
☐ c. He collapsed, the victim of a stroke

29. What is the current name of the boulevard that, between 1815 and 1828, was called the "boulevard de Gand"?

☐ a. The boulevard des Capucines
☐ b. The boulevard des Italiens
☐ c. The boulevard Poissonnière

30. Around the year 1900, what could one have found at 47 rue de Richelieu?

☐ a. A telescope lens factory
☐ b. A restaurant for single women
☐ c. A moustache hairdresser

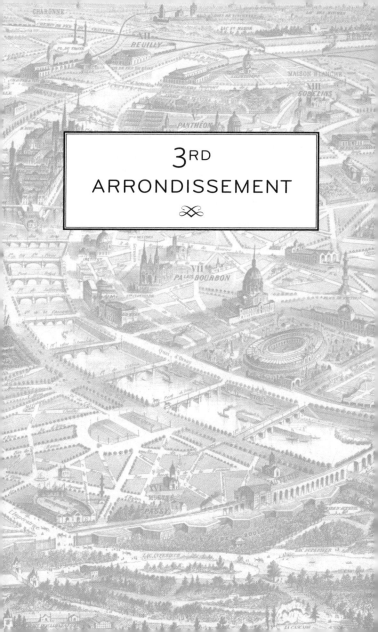

3RD
ARRONDISSEMENT

❧

1. **What is a "rambuteau"?**

   ☐ a. A coachman's whip
   ☐ b. A public urinal
   ☐ c. A gas streetlight

2. **Nicolas Flamel, the 15th century philanthropist, housed in his home agricultural workers who paid a unique rent. What did he demand from his tenants in exchange for his hospitality?**

   ☐ a. The daily recitation of two prayers
   ☐ b. The regular upkeep of the girders and chimney stacks
   ☐ c. The sweeping of his courtyard two times a day

3. **What name was formerly borne by the current passage des Ménétriers?**

   ☐ a. Rue des Jongleurs (Jugglers' Road)
   ☐ b. Rue des Troubadours (Troubadours' Road)
   ☐ c. Rue des Saltimbanques (Street Acrobats' Road)

4. **What boulevard, immortalized by Marcel Carné in *Les Enfants du Paradis*, was nicknamed "boulevard du Crime" in the 19th century?**

   ☐ a. The boulevard Saint-Martin
   ☐ b. The boulevard des Filles-du-Calvaire
   ☐ c. The boulevard du Temple

5. What is the construction date of the oldest house in Paris, situated at 51 rue de Montmorency?

   ☐ a. 1074
   ☐ b. 1407
   ☐ c. 1740

6. The roads neighboring the Conservatoire national des Arts et Métiers bear the names of scientists, industrialists and engineers. Match each with his invention:

   ☐ Conté
   ☐ The brothers
       Montgolfier
   ☐ Papin
   ☐ Réaumur
   ☐ Vaucanson
   ☐ Volta

   a. The pressure cooker
   b. The electric battery
   c. The hot air balloon
   d. The graphite pencil
   e. The alcohol thermometer
   f. The automaton

7. What was the nickname of Clément Ader's *Avion III* (Airplane III), which can be seen at the museé des Arts et Métiers?

   ☐ a. La Chauve-souris (The Bat)
   ☐ b. La Mouette (The Seagull)
   ☐ c. La Libellule (The Dragonfly)

8. What Belgian comic book artist gave the metro station Arts-et-Métiers a makeover in 1994?

   ☐ a. André Franquin
   ☐ b. François Schuiten
   ☐ c. Hergé

9. What is the speciality of the musée Cognaq-Jay, located in the hôtel de Donon?

   ☐ a. The history of wireless communication
   ☐ b. The decorative art of the 18th century
   ☐ c. The history of medieval Paris

10. Who are the "Filles du Calvaire" that figure on the street signs of the boulevard that forms the border with the 11th arrondissement?

    ☐ a. Prostitutes
    ☐ b. Martyrs
    ☐ c. Nuns

11. Who is the author of the novel *Les Filles du Calvaire*, which showcased the colorful and shady little world surrounding the cirque d'Hiver at the beginning of the 20th century?

    ☐ a. Daniel Pennac
    ☐ b. Alphonse Boudard
    ☐ c. Pierre Combescot

12. What Seine prefect does the city of Paris have to thank for the installation of two hundred fountains, the construction of the quays and several bridges, the widespread use of sidewalks and the installation of gas streetlights?

    ☐ a. Eugène Poubelle
    ☐ b. Claude Rambuteau
    ☐ c. Jules Ferry

13. What letter writer lived in a hôtel that she called her "carnavalette" (little carnival)?

   ☐ a. The comtesse de Ségur
   ☐ b. Ninon de Lenclos
   ☐ c. The marquise de Sévigné

14. Where does the name of the hôtel Salé (The Salt House), which today houses the Picasso Museum, come from?

   ☐ a. It was built by the duc de Salem
   ☐ b. Its owner made his fortune off the salt tax
   ☐ c. It was constructed on marshland, a very complicated endeavor which resulted in a steep bill (a "note salée")

15. On the 10th of September 1424, what was placed on the corner of the modern rue aux Ours?

   ☐ a. A gallows
   ☐ b. A torch holder
   ☐ c. A "mât de cocagne" (a greased pole with a goose at the top, which participants could attempt to climb to claim the goose)

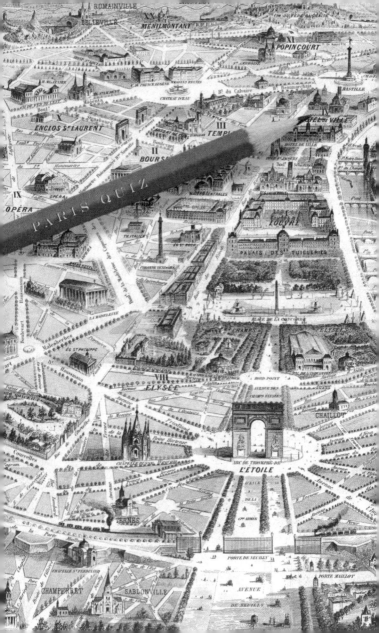

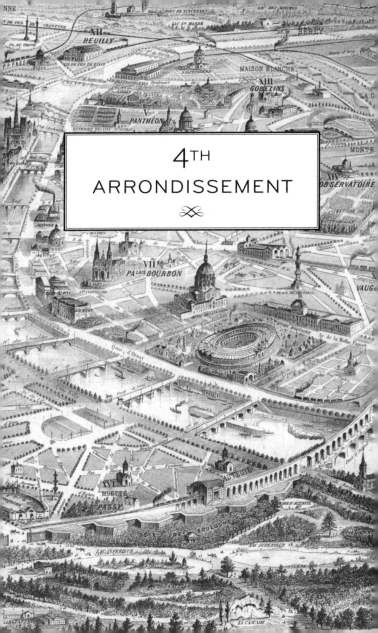

4TH
ARRONDISSEMENT

1. The Jesuit Bourdaloue preached in the église Saint-Paul-Saint-Louis. To what did he give his name, in spite of himself?

   ☐ a. A chamber pot
   ☐ b. A pastry made with almond paste
   ☐ c. A liqueur

2. How many people, on average, show up at the teller's window of the Crédit municipal (a bank primarily geared towards providing services for the poor) each day?

   ☐ a. About 50
   ☐ b. Around 300
   ☐ c. More than 600

3. What was the name of the department store opened in 1824 by Pierre Parissot on the quai aux Fleurs?

   ☐ a. Le Bon Marché
   ☐ b. La Belle Jardinière
   ☐ c. Le Joyeux Bazar

4. Why is the rue du Trésor so called?

   ☐ a. It's the former site of the Banque de France
   ☐ b. Workers found a treasure there during demolition work
   ☐ c. A dungeon, today demolished, used to house the treasury of Charles V

5. **What famous renter lived at 21 place des Vosges?**

   ☐ a. Victor Hugo
   ☐ b. Jean Giraudoux
   ☐ c. Georges Simenon

6. **An equestrian statue of Louis XIII occupies the center of the place des Vosges, but the lot of the royal horse is unenviable...why?**

   ☐ a. It's used as a slide by children in the square
   ☐ b. Its stomach is pierced by a concrete stake
   ☐ c. The animal is regularly covered in graffiti tags

7. **Why is the place des Vosges not called "place de Bretagne" or "place de Provence"?**

   ☐ a. To honor the mother of the king, who was originally from Vosges
   ☐ b. To celebrate the victory at Mirecourt
   ☐ c. Because the Vosgiens were the first to pay a new tax

8. **What is unique about the rue de Venise?**

   ☐ a. It's the narrowest road in the capital
   ☐ b. It's partially underground
   ☐ c. It's split by the canal Saint-Martin

9. **What relationship is there between the rue Nicolas-Flamel and the rue Pernelle?**

☐ a. None, besides the rhyme
☐ b. They bear the names of a husband and wife
☐ c. One turns into the other

10. **The tour Saint-Jacques is the only vestige of the église Saint-Jacques-de-la-Boucherie, dating from the Middle Ages. Why did the bell tower escape the destruction of the rest of the church during the revolution?**

☐ a. Great quantities of grenades and wheat were stored in it
☐ b. Shotgun pellets were made there
☐ c. It served as a lookout tower

11. **The name of the rue du Renard (Fox Road) was, unfortunately, trimmed over the course of time. What was the road called in the 16th century?**

☐ a. la rue du Renard-qui-Prêche (Preaching Fox Road)
☐ b. la rue du Renard-et-du-Corbeau (Fox and Crow Road)
☐ c. la rue du Renard-aux-Dents-Longues (Long Toothed Fox Road)

12. **What types of prisoners were housed in the Bastille?**

☐ a. Highwaymen and the pickpockets of the quarter
☐ b. Deserting soldiers
☐ c. Aristocrats and men of letters

13. **Where does the name of the rue du Petit-Musc come from?**

   ☐ a. From providers of white musk who had shops there
   ☐ b. From a variety of Muscat cultivated in the neighborhood
   ☐ c. From a corruption of "Pute-Y-Muse," a name which alluded to the fact that it was frequented by prostitutes

14. **Who is responsible for the obligatory alignment of buildings, the first bridge without houses on each side, and the construction of the place Dauphine and the place des Vosges?**

   ☐ a. François Mansart
   ☐ b. Jaques Lemercier
   ☐ c. Maximillien de Sully

15. **At the foot of the tour Saint-Jacques is a statue of Blaise Pascal. For a long time it was thought that the scientist engaged in research at the top of the tower: on what?**

   ☐ a. The earth's magnetic field
   ☐ b. The rotation of the earth
   ☐ c. Atmospheric pressure

16. The museums of the capital complete and lead into one another, each picking up chronologically where another leaves off. Thus the Pompidou Center houses works from a later period than those shown in the musée d'Orsay, which itself follows the collection of the Louvre. From what year are the oldest works visible in the Pompidou Center?

   ☐ a. 1870
   ☐ b. 1905
   ☐ c. 1950

17. What do the four colors (blue, green, red and yellow) of paint on the tubes in the Pompidou Center signify?

   ☐ a. They are the colors of the city of Paris
   ☐ b. Each color represents a function of the building
   ☐ c. Nothing, the colors are purely decorative

18. Which of the following hôtels, endowed with beautiful 15th century architecture, houses the Forney library, devoted to decorative arts?

   ☐ a. The hôtel de Rohan
   ☐ b. The hôtel de Sens
   ☐ c. The hôtel de Soubise

19. What May 1871 catastrophe gravely damaged Paris's Hôtel de Ville, destroying a large part of its archives?

   ☐ a. A flood of the Seine
   ☐ b. A fire
   ☐ c. An assault by Prussian artillery

20. Is there a relationship between the place de Grève (the old name for the place de l'Hôtel-de-Ville) and the expression "faire grève" (to go on strike)?

☐ a. Yes
☐ b. No

21. What is unique about the time-keeping device of the church of Saint-Louis-en-l'Île?

☐ a. It is a very old sundial made of enameled lava
☐ b. It overhangs the road like a sign
☐ c. It resembles a cuckoo clock, with a mechanical figure shooting out at a fixed hour

22. What used to be located under the buildings of the Garde républicaine, along the boulevard Henri-IV?

☐ a. A mushroom farm fed with horse dung
☐ b. The private cellar of the king, where exceptional vintages were aged
☐ c. An immense reservoir of drinkable water

23. The Île de la Cité currently has about twenty roads. How many were there in the 17th century, before it was completely redrafted by Haussmann?

☐ a. 100
☐ b. 350
☐ c. 500

24. How did Xavier Ruel, who founded BHV in 1856, decide on the location of his shop?

    ☐ a. Blindly, throwing a dart on a map of Paris
    ☐ b. He started construction on the site where he met his wife
    ☐ c. By testing beforehand for the best sales location in the capital

25. Which quay of the île Saint-Louis used to be called the "quai des Balcons" (the Quay of Balconies) due to its great number of balconies open at midday?

    ☐ a. The quai d'Anjou
    ☐ b. The quai de Bourbon
    ☐ c. The quai de Béthune

26. What venerable room has the church of Saint-Merri housed since 1331?

    ☐ a. The oldest altar in the capital
    ☐ b. The oldest baptistery in the capital
    ☐ c. The oldest bell tower

27. During what era were the Île Notre-Dame and the Île aux Vaches linked to form the Île Saint-Louis?

    ☐ a. The 16th century
    ☐ b. The 17th century
    ☐ c. The 18th century

28. **What location so seduced Henri IV that he used it as an inspiration during the construction of the place Royale (now the place des Vosges)?**

    ☐ a. The arenas in Nîmes
    ☐ b. Armagnac's place de Labastide
    ☐ c. The pont du Gard

29. **On the 13th of March 1970, the comedian Jean Yanne was stopped by the police in the place du Marché-Sainte-Catherine. Why?**

    ☐ a. He was stealing wheel clamps
    ☐ b. He put graffiti on a wall
    ☐ c. He struck a ticket machine

30. **What appeared in 1640 on the rue Saint-Martin?**

    ☐ a. The first taxi business
    ☐ b. The first system of gutters, to recuperate rainwater
    ☐ c. The first eight-story apartment building

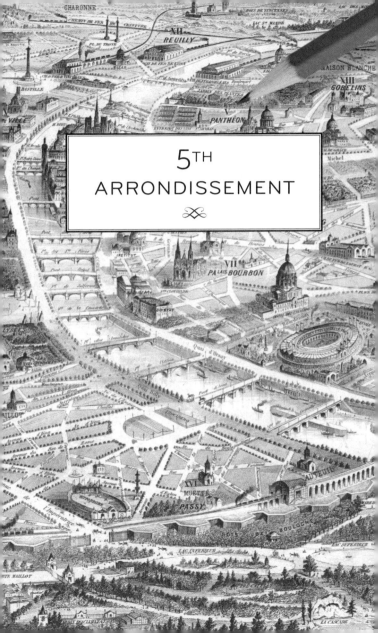

5TH
ARRONDISSEMENT

1. Who was the first King to make Paris the seat of his kingdom?

   ☐ a. Saint Louis
   ☐ b. Clovis
   ☐ c. Charlemagne

2. Who was the only woman judged worthy of resting eternally under the dome of the Panthéon alongside approximately 60 great men?

   ☐ a. Marie Curie
   ☐ b. Simone de Beauvoir
   ☐ c. Flora Tristan

3. What artist is responsible for the sundial inlaid in the wall of 27 rue Saint-Jacques?

   ☐ a. Salvador Dalí
   ☐ b. Hector Guimard
   ☐ c. Jean Tinguely

4. The Val-de-Grâce was born of a wish. Anne of Austria promised to have the church built if her request was granted. What was the queen praying for?

   ☐ a. The birth of a son and royal heir
   ☐ b. The safe return of her royal spouse from a crusade
   ☐ c. The death of her royal spouse on a crusade

5. **The Panthéon (formerly the church of Sainte-Geneviève), like the Val-de-Grâce, was born of the granting of a royal wish, this time that of Louis XV. What did he wish?**

☐ a. The birth of an heir
☐ b. A cure
☐ c. The assurance of a victory

6. **On the current rue Jean-de-Beauvais is the workshop of the Estiennes, humanist printers during the Renaissance. On the door of their workshop was affixed a poster promising a tidy reward. To whom was it addressed?**

☐ a. To whomever could provide them with a paper resistant to the effects of time and mold
☐ b. To whomever could recover a precious illuminated manuscript that had been stolen from them
☐ c. To whomever could find a misprint in a book they had printed

7. **What is the former name of the current rue de Parcheminerie (Parchment Factory Road)?**

☐ a. Rue des Imprimeurs (Printers' Road)
☐ b. Rue des Écrivains (Writers' Road)
☐ c. Rue des Gratte-Papier (Paper Scratchers' Road)

8. **What is Bilipo?**

☐ a. A library specializing in police literature
☐ b. A range of street vacuuming machines
☐ c. A team of professional climbers charged with washing the glass sides of skyscrapers

9. **Why is the Latin Quarter so named?**

    ☐ a. Because its universities attracted numerous Italian students
    ☐ b. Because teaching was conducted in Latin during the Middle Ages
    ☐ c. Because the hill on which it is situated used to be called the mont Palatin (the Palantine Hill)

10. **Who is the patron saint of Paris?**

    ☐ a. Saint Anne
    ☐ b. Saint Cécile
    ☐ c. Saint Geneviève

11. **The saint organized the resistance of Parisians against the threat of invasion and valiantly opposed the abandoning of the city to barbarians. Who was threatening Paris in 451 AD?**

    ☐ a. Franks led by Childéric
    ☐ b. Huns led by Attila
    ☐ c. Visigoths led by Théodoric

12. **The little théâtre de la Huchette, on the street of the same name, holds a record: they've been performing the same show since 1957. Which?**

    ☐ a. Jean Cocteau's *Les Enfants terribles*
    ☐ b. Eugène Ionesco's *La Cantatrice chauve*
    ☐ c. Molière's *Tartuffe*

13. **At the musée national du Moyen Âge a set of six tapestries is exhibited: the famous *Lady and the Unicorn*. What do the tapestries show?**

   ☐ a. Six episodes from the crusade of the Duke of Normandy
   ☐ b. The five senses and a motto
   ☐ c. Jousting matches and a hymn to platonic love sung by a troubadour

14. **What is a "robinier"?**

   ☐ a. An endemic species of woodpigeon
   ☐ b. A worker charged with the upkeep of public fountains
   ☐ c. A tree with white flowers

15. **The church of Saint-Étienne-du-Mont contains the last rood screen in Paris. What exactly is a rood screen?**

   ☐ a. An open bell tower
   ☐ b. A corridor above the nave
   ☐ c. A massive wood altar

16. **During what period were the arènes de Lutèce erected?**

   ☐ a. The 1st century BC
   ☐ b. The beginning of the 2nd century
   ☐ c. The end of the 6th century

17. **Why did Napoleon III have the original layout of the boulevard Saint-Michel shifted, so that it now deviates at a slight angle from the north-south axis?**

    ☐ a. To avoid destroying the antique thermal baths of Cluny
    ☐ b. So that the spire of Sainte-Chapelle appears in its view
    ☐ c. Purely on a whim, as Napoleon III knew nothing of city planning

18. **What were the long billy clubs of the riot police nicknamed in May 1968?**

    ☐ a. "Bâtons de berger" (shepherds' crooks)
    ☐ b. "Bidules" (Thingamajigs)
    ☐ c. "Barracudas"

19. **In the film *La Traversée de Paris*, what character (brought to life by Louis de Funès) did actor Jean Gabin cry the name of at the top of his lungs outside of 45 rue de Poliveau?**

    ☐ a. Jambier
    ☐ b. Mandrin
    ☐ c. Grangil

20. **What films were partially shot in the pool at 19 rue du Pontoise?**

    ☐ a. *Bleu*
    ☐ b. *Nelly et M. Arnaud*
    ☐ c. *La Discrète*

21. **The abbé de L'Épée was a benefactor. But of whom?**

    ☐ a. The blind
    ☐ b. Deaf mutes
    ☐ c. Foundlings

22. **In 1836 the church of Saint-Cosme was demolished to make room on the boulevard Saint-Michel. The construction unearthed remains from an old cemetery adjoining the church. What was peculiar about it?**

    ☐ a. It was an animal cemetery
    ☐ b. It was a cemetery for clergy
    ☐ c. It was a cemetery for hunchbacks

23. **What postmortem honor did Louis Pasteur and Charles de Gaulle refuse in advance?**

    ☐ a. The Nobel Prize
    ☐ b. Burial in the Panthéon
    ☐ c. Statues celebrating their glory

24. **What were the "moffettes" whose memory the rue Mouffetard evokes?**

    ☐ a. Women of little virtue
    ☐ b. Pestilent odors
    ☐ c. Honeycombs

25. **On the front of what building can one read the names of 810 writers and scientists engraved in stone?**

    ☐ a. The Panthéon
    ☐ b. The Sorbonne
    ☐ c. The Sainte-Geneviève Library

26. What metro station evokes a mathematician who created descriptive geometry?

   ☐ a. Place-Monge
   ☐ b. Censier-Daubenton
   ☐ c. Jussieu

27. What naturalist introduced Merino sheep to France?

   ☐ a. Buffon
   ☐ b. Censier
   ☐ c. Daubenton

28. The mineralogy gallery of the Muséum national d'histoire naturelle contains an impressive collection of giant crystals. What is the weight of the heaviest among them?

   ☐ a. 40 kg
   ☐ b. 400 kg
   ☐ c. 4,000 kg

29. What is unique about the basin Pastoral, a fountain situated at the end of the rue Soufflot, in front of the principal entry to the Luxembourg Garden?

   ☐ a. It flows through both the summer and winter
   ☐ b. The water it spouts has a light green tint
   ☐ c. It is equipped with an audio anti-pigeon system

30. What type of market was held in the place Maubert during the 19th century?

   ☐ a. A cigarette butt exchange
   ☐ b. A used clothing market
   ☐ c. A skins market (rabbit, fox, etc.)

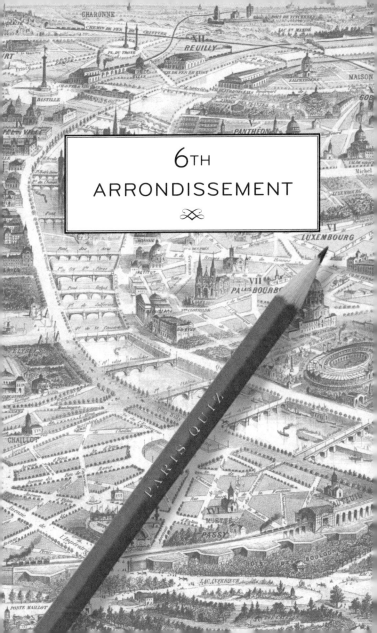

6TH
ARRONDISSEMENT

1. **What are inhabitants of Saint-Germain-des-Prés called?**

    ☐ a. Prégermaniques
    ☐ b. Germanopratins
    ☐ c. Germinois

2. **Where does the name of the café des Deux-Magots come from?**

    ☐ a. From a corruption of "vieux mégots" (old cigarette butts), which littered the floor of the establishment
    ☐ b. From two bags full of gold pieces, discovered in a well, which allowed the founder of the café to open his establishment
    ☐ c. From two oriental statues of magi ("magots"), on display in what used to be a novelty shop

3. **What color is the dress of members of an Académie (the prestigious learning societies which comprise the Institut de France)?**

    ☐ a. Green
    ☐ b. Blue
    ☐ c. Black

4. **The rue Jean-Bart evokes:**

    ☐ a. A "flibustier"
    ☐ b. A pirate
    ☐ c. A corsair

5. How many Académies does the Institut de France house?

   ☐ a. 4
   ☐ b. 5
   ☐ c. 6

6. The sword of each Académie member is personalized with symbols of their work. Thus, Jean Cocteau's was decorated with a profile of Oedipus Rex, while commander Cousteau's used crystal, a material that is transparent like water. What motif decorated the sword of biologist Jean Rostand?

   ☐ a. Toads
   ☐ b. Test tubes
   ☐ c. A cluster of molecules

7. The palais Conti houses the hôtel de la Monnaie (the Paris mint) where all types of medals are struck. What is the term for the "heads" side of a coin or a medal?

   ☐ a. The underside
   ☐ b. The obverse
   ☐ c. The verso

8. A certain 18th-century philosopher and regular of Procope once responded to those who told him that coffee was a slow killer: "I'm obliged to believe in its slowness since this makes forty years I've been drinking it." Who was this wise thinker?

   ☐ a. Beaumarchais
   ☐ b. Voltaire
   ☐ c. Diderot

9. At 36 rue du Vaugirard, a standard marble meter is sealed in the wall of the Agency of Weights and Measures. It was — like many others in all the villages of France — placed on a highly trafficked road in order to familiarize the people with the new unit of measure. During what era did the meter replace the old units of measurement?

   ☐ a. During the revolution
   ☐ b. Under the empire
   ☐ c. During the restoration

10. The distant history of the Luxembourg Garden is the basis for what popular expression?

   ☐ a. "To pay with monkey money" (To make excuses and jokes instead of paying a debt)
   ☐ b. "To live at the vauvert devil's" (To live in the middle of nowhere)
   ☐ c. "To spin a bad thread" (To catch a bad break)

11. Of the four following establishments, which one cannot be called "germanopratin"?

   ☐ a. Les Deux-Magots
   ☐ b. La Closerie des Lilas
   ☐ c. La brasserie Lipp
   ☐ d. Le Café de Flore

12. The Zadkine Museum, on the rue d'Assas, houses the works of Ossip Zadkine. In what art did he distinguish himself?

☐ a. Sculpture
☐ b. Painting
☐ c. Photography

13. What establishment was the first lycée (the French equivalent of a high school) to welcome girls in 1883?

☐ a. The lycée Fénelon
☐ b. The lycée Louis-le-Grand
☐ c. The lycée Henri IV

14. What writer installed himself for three straight days in the Café de la Mairie, at the corner of the rue des Canettes and the place Saint-Suplice, to write *Tentative d'épuisement d'un lieu parisien*?

☐ a. Georges Perec
☐ b. Maurice G. Dantec
☐ c. Michel Houellebecq

15. Around the year 1900, the crossroads of the rue Bernard-Palissy and the rue du Sabot was the theatre of what sort of test?

☐ a. A driving aptitude test for four horse teams
☐ b. A balance competition among water carriers
☐ c. A masculine elegance competition

16. What material does the Belle Époque–style sculpture affixed to a section of wall in the square Félix-Desrulles, along the boulevard Saint-Germain, pay homage to?

   ☐ a. Ceramic
   ☐ b. Glass
   ☐ c. Wood

17. What does the word "odéon" mean in Greek?

   ☐ a. Circle of wind
   ☐ b. Public place
   ☐ c. A room where one sings

18. How did the physicist Pierre Curie die, on April 19, 1906, on the corner of the rue Dauphine and the quai des grands-Augustins?

   ☐ a. He was the victim of muggers
   ☐ b. He was struck by a heart attack
   ☐ c. He was run over by a car

19. Who was Mabillon?

   ☐ a. A composer of operas
   ☐ b. A monk who was passionate about diplomacy
   ☐ c. A portrait artist

20. What does the fontaine du Québec (situated in the place du Québec) resemble?

   ☐ a. A trapper's hut
   ☐ b. The ice cracking on a frozen river in spring
   ☐ c. A stylized caribou

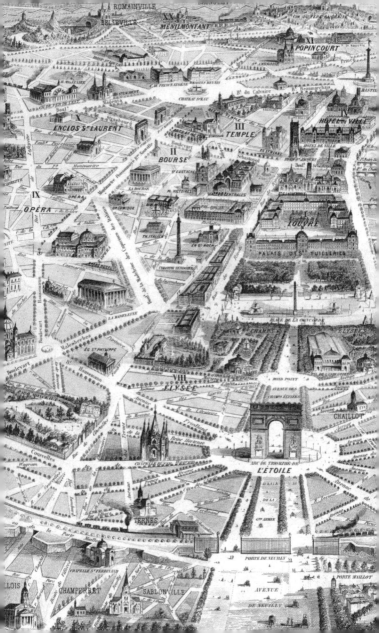

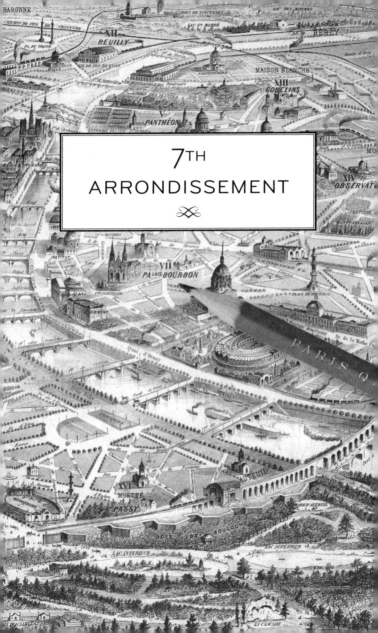

7TH
ARRONDISSEMENT

1. In 1800, the Parisian sewers essentially consisted of a 20 km network. Over what distance do their passages run today?

   ☐ a. 650 km
   ☐ b. 1,800 km
   ☐ c. 2,400 km

2. Réné Laennec was the father of what medical instrument?

   ☐ a. The stethoscope
   ☐ b. The lancet
   ☐ c. The hemostat

3. What do the four legs of the tour Eiffel rest on?

   ☐ a. Caissons filled with water
   ☐ b. Caissons filled with oil
   ☐ c. Caissons filled with concrete

4. Two steps from the metro Vaneau, a chapel houses a mummy! Whose?

   ☐ a. Henri IV's
   ☐ b. Jean-François Champollion's
   ☐ c. Saint Vincent de Paul's

5. How many years pass between the application of each new coat of paint to the Eiffel Tower?

   ☐ a. 5 years
   ☐ b. 7 years
   ☐ c. 10 years

6. **How many years did it take before the loan that financed the construction of the Eiffel Tower was paid off by its takings?**

   ☐ a. 1 month
   ☐ b. 1 year
   ☐ c. 10 years

7. **In 1870 the Prussians were at the gates of the capital. How were the Parisians able to prevent the statue of Napoleon I (which is today located in the cour des Invalides) from falling into the hands of the traditional enemies of the Empire?**

   ☐ a. They covered it in plaster to disguise it as a Roman goddess
   ☐ b. They submerged it in the Seine
   ☐ c. They hoisted it into a tree, hiding it in the foliage

8. **The Musée des Plans-Reliefs displays approximately one hundred scale models of cities and French sites made in the 18th and 19th centuries. What were they used for?**

   ☐ a. They were put to military ends, used for a better mastery of strategic locations
   ☐ b. They were meant for the edification of Parisians by showing them provinces and freshly conquered territories
   ☐ c. They had no ends but artistic ones, serving as models for painters chronicling the sites

9. What quantity of gold was necessary to re-gild the dome of the Invalides in 1989?

☐ a. 1.265 kg
☐ b. 12.65 kg
☐ c. 126.5 kg

10. From 1925 to 1936, an automobile manufacturer used the Eiffel Tower as a giant billboard, putting his name in giant, luminous, multicolored letters on the four sides of the monument. Who was it?

☐ a. André Citroën
☐ b. Louis Renault
☐ c. Armand Peugeot

11. To whom does the tour Eiffel belong?

☐ a. The State
☐ b. The city of Paris
☐ c. A private company

12. The current La Pagode cinema was the site of a humorous mishap in the 1930s. The Peking government, tempted by the oriental curves of the then for-sale building, presented itself as a candidate to install its embassy there. It sent a delegation of diplomats... who quickly turned on their heels. What did the visitors see that was so shocking?

☐ a. Frescoes showing the Chinese army being routed by Japanese adversaries
☐ b. Murals illustrating the boldest positions of the *Kama Sutra*
☐ c. None of the rules of feng shui had been followed

13. **What do the collections of the musée Valentin-Haüy evoke?**

☐ a. The saga of the gold rush
☐ b. The teaching of the blind
☐ c. Progress in the field of biochemistry

14. **What do missionary monks traditionally do before leaving to evangelize in far-off lands?**

☐ a. They light a candle for Saint Thomas Aquinas, in the church of the same name
☐ b. They meditate before the relics of their martyred brothers in the chapelle de la Mission
☐ c. They plant a tree in the jardin des Missions étrangères, one of the largest in Paris

15. **The Eiffel Tower, constructed for the World's Fair of 1889, was supposed to be demolished shortly thereafter. What saved it, in 1909?**

☐ a. Its aesthetic qualities, praised by three hundred artists in a petition
☐ b. Its technical, scientific and military usefulness
☐ c. The greed of a private company, which had already glimpsed a juicy profit in it

16. **To what climatic change is the Eiffel Tower most susceptible?**

☐ a. Sun
☐ b. Cold
☐ c. Wind

17. The hotel de Salm, situated at 2 rue de la Légion d'Honneur, houses a national museum devoted to the Légion d'honneur and other chivalric orders. To what English order does the motto: "Honni soit qui mal y pense" ("Shame upon him who thinks evil upon it," in Old French) belong?

☐ a. The Most Noble Order of the Garter
☐ b. The Order of the Golden Fleece
☐ c. The Equestrian Order of the Holy Sepulcher

18. What animal sculptures greet visitors to the musée d'Orsay?

☐ a. A unicorn, a sphinx and a dragon
☐ b. A giraffe, a lion and a peacock
☐ c. A rhinoceros, a horse and an elephant

19. Among the most famous of Rodin's works shown at his museum is the renowned *Thinker*. Who is he and what is he thinking about?

☐ a. Dante, thinking of his poem *The Inferno*
☐ b. Balzac, fine-tuning the psychological profile of one of his heroes
☐ c. Apollo, asking himself how to seduce the nymph Coronis

20. What nickname, borrowed from the language of ornithology, is given to the spot occupied by the president of the National Assembly?

☐ a. The plumage
☐ b. The perch
☐ c. The henhouse

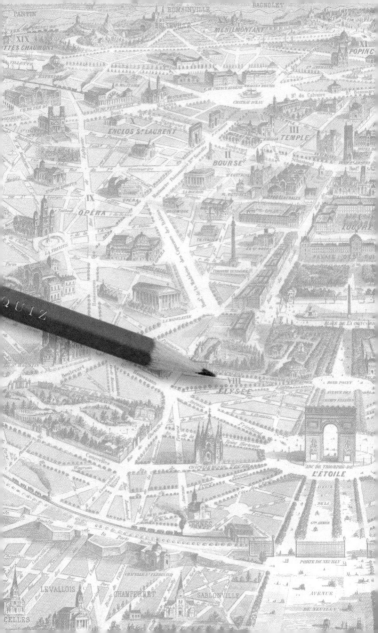

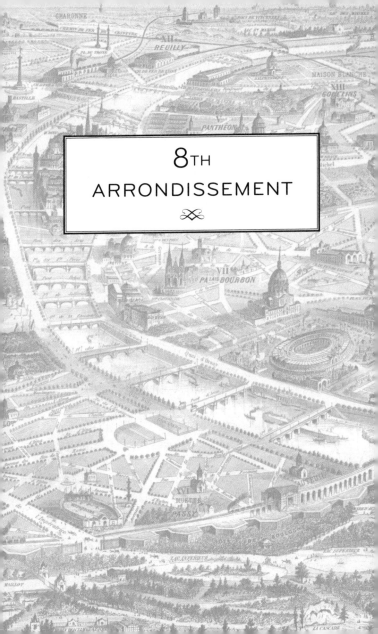

8TH
ARRONDISSEMENT
❦

1. **What did the Champs-Élysées look like from 1833 to 1860?**

   ☐ a. A racetrack
   ☐ b. A battlefield
   ☐ c. A fairgrounds

2. **What merchants were the first to install themselves along the Champs-Élysées?**

   ☐ a. Men's hat sellers
   ☐ b. Sellers of equestrian supplies
   ☐ c. Perfume sellers

3. **In the 1970s, a rich American tourist was the victim of an incredible scandal. A crook got him to believe that he had been charged by the state with the sale of a certain monument, and reached a deal with the American. A few days later, the American dispatched a crane to the place de la Concorde...and was surprised to see the police object to the taking of an object he held the title to. What monument did he want to cart off?**

   ☐ a. The Obelisk
   ☐ b. The Horses of Marly
   ☐ c. The rostral columns

4. **Where did the traditional July 14th military review take place, before moving onto the Champs-Élysées?**

   ☐ a. On the Champ-de-Mars
   ☐ b. On the hippodrome de Longchamp
   ☐ c. Nowhere, it started on the Champs-Élysées

5. The Miromesnil metro station bears the name of a magistrate who, in 1774, abolished "preparatory questioning". What was "preparatory questioning"?

    ☐ a. An entrance exam to the National School of Medicine
    ☐ b. A euphemism used to refer to torture inflicted on prisoners
    ☐ c. An identity check imposed on all foreigners entering the capital

6. With what frequency is the unknown soldier's flame lit, to the sound of a bugle?

    ☐ a. Every evening
    ☐ b. Every Sunday morning
    ☐ c. Every November 11th

7. What is the watchman in charge of the upkeep and surveillance of the memorial flame burning under the Arc de triomphe supposed to do if, by some misfortune, a gust of wind or a treacherous rain should put it out?

    ☐ a. Obviously, rush to relight it as quickly as possible
    ☐ b. Immediately refer it to a committee, which will organize a ceremony to relight it right away
    ☐ c. It can't be put out, a clever device assures a permanent flame

8. How were Nélie Jacquemart and her husband Édouard André able to gather the exceptional collection of nearly five thousand pieces of furniture, objects and paintings destined to decorate their sumptuous town house?

☐ a. Indefatigable globetrotters, they traveled the world for 20 years
☐ b. The rich patrons assured the subsistence of a number of artists who reimbursed them in kind
☐ c. Thirteen successive inheritances permitted the independently wealthy couple to satisfy their common passion

9. What color are all the illuminated signs on the Champs-Élysées?

☐ a. Blue
☐ b. Green
☐ c. White

10. What are the inhabitants of the Champs-Élysées called?

☐ a. Élyséens
☐ b. Champélyséens
☐ c. Élysiens

11. **For what reason was the marquise du Marbeuf, who had a hotel on the Champs-Élysées, guillotined in 1794?**

    ☐ a. For not having wanted, out of vanity, to wear the Phrygian Bonnet
    ☐ b. For having housed the royal family for one night
    ☐ c. For having sowed alfalfa in her park

12. **What nickname is given to collectors who swap, sell and research stamps, postal materials, post cards and phone cards in the Carré Marigny?**

    ☐ a. "Pieds-nicklés" (Nickel feet)
    ☐ b. "Pieds-humides" (Wet feet)
    ☐ c. "Pieds-de-grue" (Crane feet)

13. **What very chic Triangle d'or avenue bears the name of the author of the maxim: "On the highest throne in the world, we're still only ever sitting on our own bottoms"?**

    ☐ a. George-V
    ☐ b. Montaigne
    ☐ c. François I

14. **What was the Champs-Élysées paved with from 1886 to 1938?**

    ☐ a. Little blocks of granite
    ☐ b. Wooden pavers
    ☐ c. Cemented gravel

15. **What type of urinals did early 20th century Parisians see appear along the Champs- Élysées?**

    ☐ a. Urinals for women, called "dalmatiennes"
    ☐ b. Moving urinals with wheels
    ☐ c. Art nouveau–style urinals

16. **In what way is the Madeleine different from other churches?**

    ☐ a. It lacks a bell tower
    ☐ b. It isn't oriented to the east
    ☐ c. It has no altar

17. **Why were the parades of July 14, 1921 and July 14, 1929 cancelled at the last minute?**

    ☐ a. The heat was too strong
    ☐ b. A violent hailstorm occurred, followed by a gale
    ☐ c. Grand-scale sabotage immobilized floats and parade vehicles

18. **Who first had the idea of a parade on the Champs-Élysées?**

    ☐ a. Napoleon I
    ☐ b. Louis-Philippe
    ☐ c. General de Gaulle

19. **Where does the cabaret du Lido get its name?**

    ☐ a. From a Venetian beach
    ☐ b. From a Roman goddess
    ☐ c. From a Sicilian singer

20. **Why did the establishment of the fashion boutique Rosemonde on the "most beautiful avenue in the world" spark a heated debate within the Champs-Élysées committee in 1932?**

☐ a. Its dresses weren't expensive enough, compromising the luxurious image of the avenue

☐ b. Because its above-the-knee skirts were judged outrageously short

☐ c. Because it offered the first pants and swimsuits for women, indecent in the eyes of its contemporaries

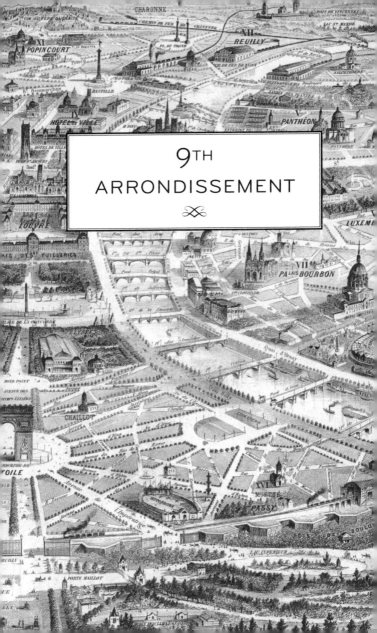

9TH
ARRONDISSEMENT

1. **What is the nickname of the commissioners who officiate in the Drouot salesroom?**

    ☐ a.   Red collars
    ☐ b.   Charm wearers
    ☐ c.   Brogues

2. **What was the name of the first wax museum, which opened to the public at the end of the 18th century on the boulevard du Temple?**

    ☐ a.   The Cave of Thieves
    ☐ b.   The Illusory
    ☐ c.   The Human Menagerie

3. **What misadventure did the musée Grévin's wax figure of Fernandel suffer, in its Don Camillo costume?**

    ☐ a.   The reprisals of a militant communist who, furious to see that Peppone wasn't on display, took revenge by splashing the poor Don Camillo with red ink!
    ☐ b.   An anonymous attempt at bewitchment by black magic
    ☐ c.   The affectionate but overly violent attack of an admirer

4. **What popped up out of the ground at the intersection of the boulevards Saint-Denis and Sébastopol on May 5, 1923?**

    ☐ a.   The first newspaper kiosk
    ☐ b.   The first traffic light
    ☐ c.   The first automatic public toilet

5. **Why did Napoleon III suddenly decide to have a new Opera built in Paris in January of 1858?**

☐ a. To satisfy the caprice of the Empress Eugénie
☐ b. Because the old Opera on the rue Le Peletier no longer met safety standards
☐ c. To accommodate a grandiose staging of a new Jules Massenet opera

6. **How much does the great chandelier hung above the performance hall of the Garnier Opéra weigh?**

☐ a. 600 kg
☐ b. 1.6 tons
☐ c. 6 tons

7. **What happened at the Opéra Garnier on May 20, 1896, during a performance of *Faust*?**

☐ a. The performance hall's chandelier became unhooked
☐ b. A fire ravaged the stage and the forestage
☐ c. A spectator, taken with a bout of dementia, killed seven people

8. **Where does the name of the Nouvelle Athènes quarter come from?**

☐ a. Paris's first Olympic pool was built there, in 1932
☐ b. From its proximity to a theatre called "The New Athens"
☐ c. From the architecture of the apartment buildings, inspired by the ancient Greek repertoire

9. **It is rare for a church to be without a bell tower. Why does the église Saint-Eugène-Sainte-Cécile lack one?**

   ☐ a. Gifts from generous parishioners strangely petered out, and no money remained to complete the church
   ☐ b. It was designed that way, so as not to upset the tranquility of the quarter
   ☐ c. The tower, destroyed during the bombings of the Second World War, was not rebuilt

10. **Why did the prince Louis Napoléon Bonaparte have the cité Napoléon built in 1849?**

    ☐ a. As a housing project for workers
    ☐ b. In order to offer artists the best working conditions possible
    ☐ c. To use as a model prison where each prisoner had his own cell

11. **On the 28th of December 1895 the first paid showing of the Lumière brothers' motion picture projector took place in a room of the Grand Café Capucines. What was the subject of the short film?**

    ☐ a. Workers leaving the Lumière factories
    ☐ b. A Deauville beach in the middle of the summer
    ☐ c. Acrobats perched on unicycles

12. **What can one find at 65 boulevard de Clichy, in the middle of Pigalle?**

    ☐ a. A chapel
    ☐ b. A cinema for children
    ☐ c. A Zen garden

13. In what metro station was François Truffaut's film
Le Dernier Métro (The Last Metro) partially shot?

☐ a. Anvers
☐ b. Pigalle
☐ c. Blanche

14. Why is place Blanche (White Square) so named?

☐ a. Facing directly south, it is always very bright
☐ b. It used to be crossed by plasterers' carts
☐ c. Its real name is place Blanche-de-Castille
     (Castillian White Square), but it was shortened
     in usage

15. Who is the author of the poem "Hymn to place
Blanche under snow"?

☐ a. Francis Blanche
☐ b. Charles Cros
☐ c. Serge Gainsbourg

16. The place Saint-Georges is adorned with a fountain at
its center, surmounted by a bust of Gavrani. Who was
Gavrani?

☐ a. A caricaturist
☐ b. An alpinist
☐ c. An aviator

17. What Parisian character does the Julien Auguste Lorieux sculpture placed in the square Montholon in 1925 whimsically evoke?

☐ a. The urchin
☐ b. The lorette (a mistress of multiple lovers)
☐ c. The catherinette (a woman unmarried by the age of 25)

18. What Parisian specialty first appeared in 1909, simultaneously on the rue de Mogador and the rue de la Chaussée-d'Antin?

☐ a. Roasted chestnuts
☐ b. The jambon-beurre (a ham and butter sandwich)
☐ c. One-way traffic

19. What landed on the roof of the Galeries Lafayette on January 19, 1919?

☐ a. A group of storks
☐ b. A hot air balloon
☐ c. An airplane

20. What did Georges Sand, Gustave Courbet and Honoré Daumier refuse together?

☐ a. That a statue be devoted to them while they were still alive
☐ b. To be decorated with the Légion d'honneur
☐ c. Seats in the Académie des Beaux-Arts

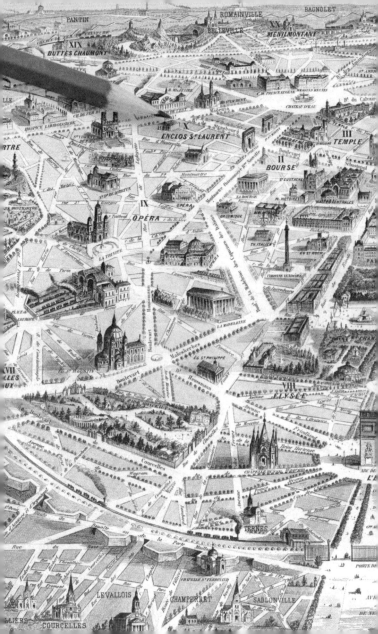

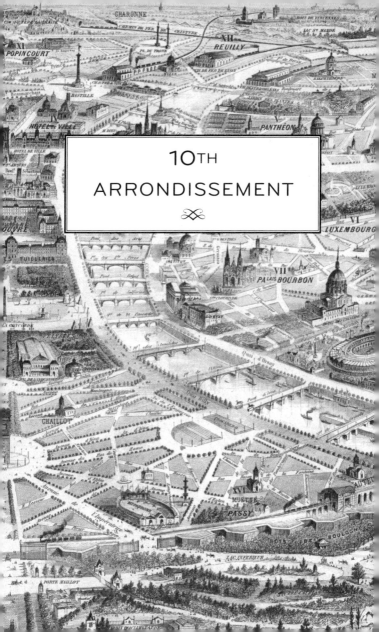

10TH

ARRONDISSEMENT

❦

1. **What tragic event plunged the Couronnes metro station into mourning on August 10, 1903?**

    ☐ a. An attack by an anarchist league
    ☐ b. The collision of two trains
    ☐ c. A fire

2. **Who was Laribosière, whose name is now born by a hospital?**

    ☐ a. A Seine prefect
    ☐ b. A renowned surgeon
    ☐ c. A wealthy countess

3. **What professionals come to stock up on material necessary to the exercise of their profession, in the boutiques of the passage de l'Industrie?**

    ☐ a. Dentists and dental technicians
    ☐ b. Hairdressers and wig makers
    ☐ c. Cooks and hoteliers

4. **What are artists who make hand fans called?**

    ☐ a. Éventiers
    ☐ b. Éventaillistes
    ☐ c. Éventailleurs

5. **How many locks are there in the canal Saint-Martin?**

    ☐ a. 5
    ☐ b. 9
    ☐ c. 12

6. How long does it take a boat to cross a lock?

   ☐ a. 5 minutes
   ☐ b. 10 minutes
   ☐ c. 20 minutes

7. Why is one of the canal Saint-Martin's locks called "the lock of the dead"?

   ☐ a. It is bridged by a high gangway popular among those attempting suicide
   ☐ b. It evokes the memory of an old gallows
   ☐ c. The lock's name actually comes from a corruption of the French word for "Moors"

8. On what footbridge over the canal Saint-Martin did Arletty issue her famous retort: "Atmosphère, atmosphère...est-ce que j'ai une gueule d'atmosphère?"

   ☐ a. The passerelle Bichat
   ☐ b. The passerelle Dieu
   ☐ c. The passerelle de la Douane

9. During what era did the passage Brady become predominantly Indian and Pakistani?

   ☐ a. The 1960s
   ☐ b. The 1970s
   ☐ c. The 1980s

10. According to the wish of what sovereign were the porte Saint-Denis and the porte Saint-Martin built?

☐ a. Louis XIV
☐ b. Charles X
☐ c. Napoleon I

11. Saint-Martin is the name of a boulevard, but also of a phantom metro station, that can be briefly glimpsed between the Strasbourg-Saint-Denis and République stations (on lines 8 and 9). Closed in 1939, at the beginning of the war, it was never reopened. Why?

☐ a. The roof over the platform was at risk of collapsing
☐ b. It was never finished due to lack of means
☐ c. It was too close to the nearest stations

12. Why did Parisians crowd under the windows of 51 rue du Chabrol during August 1899?

☐ a. They were coming to listen to a preacher
☐ b. They were following the evolution of the siege of an apartment building taken over by a group of individuals
☐ c. They were attending the first tests of the optic telegraph

13. How wide is the narrowest building front in Paris, at 39 rue du Château-d'Eau?

☐ a. 1.2 m
☐ b. 2.3 m
☐ c. 3.2 m

14. **Why is Jacques Bonsergent honored with a metro station?**

    ☐ a. For his courage
    ☐ b. For his scientific work
    ☐ c. For his lithography

15. **What type of castings can be viewed at the Saint-Louis Hospital's musée des Moulages (Museum of Castings)?**

    ☐ a. Busts of famous doctors and men of science
    ☐ b. Signed casts used to set the limbs of the famous
    ☐ c. Wax castings of dermatological and venereal diseases

16. **Why is the gare du Nord, built by Hittorff, set back from the boulevard de Magenta and shifted in relation to the gare de l'Est?**

    ☐ a. Out of fear that runaway trains might charge down the boulevard
    ☐ b. Because of Haussmann's desire to annoy Hittorff
    ☐ c. Due to a geological constraint

17. **What can be seen at 18 rue de Paradis?**

    ☐ a. An art nouveau caretaker's lodge
    ☐ b. A pair of cherubs fluttering on a stone porch, representing heaven
    ☐ c. A bistro called L'Enfer (Hell)

18. **What proud title can the Saint-Louis hospital claim?**

☐ a. It was the first building in France lit with gas
☐ b. It was the first hospital equipped with elevators
☐ c. It was the first to offer individual rooms to the ill

19. **What was there to be found, during the Middle Ages, between the current rue de la Grange-aux-Belles and place du Colonel-Fabien?**

☐ a. A gallows
☐ b. A donkey market
☐ c. A fortified wall

20. **Which of the following is spanned by the rue de l'Aqueduc?**

☐ a. The canal Saint-Martin
☐ b. The tracks of the gare de l'Est
☐ c. The gardens of the Lariboisière hospital

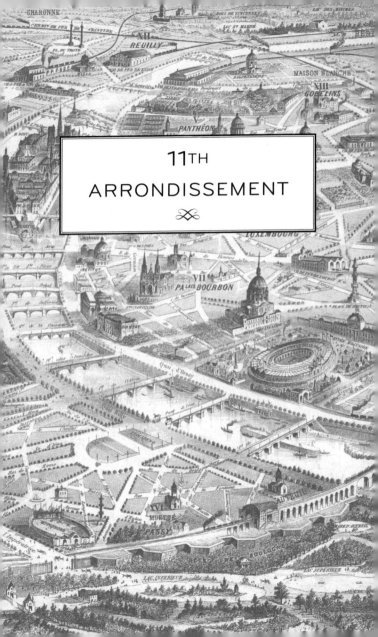

11TH
ARRONDISSEMENT

1. **What curiosity can be found in the jardin Émile-Gallé (formerly the jardin de la cité Beauharnais)?**

   ☐ a. A rose garden dedicated to Josephine
   ☐ b. A pyramid of greenery onto which a waterfall falls
   ☐ c. A horizontal sundial

2. **What is unique about the two caryatids that surround the coat of arms of Paris above the clock on the façade of the town hall of the 11th arrondissement?**

   ☐ a. They have children's bodies
   ☐ b. They are the only statues that can be seen crying
   ☐ c. They're maliciously thumbing their noses at passersby

3. **Whose memory does the metro station Richard-Lenoir evoke?**

   ☐ a. A deputy Lenoir, whose first name was Richard
   ☐ b. Two associates: M. Richard and M. Lenoir
   ☐ c. A certain Richard, an artist, nicknamed "le Noir" (the black)

4. **What did Monsieur Oberkampf work on?**

   ☐ a. The development of the aspirin tablet
   ☐ b. Making printed cloths
   ☐ c. Popularizing the use of the electric battery

5. Rue Coriolis pays homage to an engineer who worked on centrifugal forces — since deemed Coriolis forces — linked to the rotation of the earth. He discovered, notably, that the water that empties from a sink doesn't swirl in the same direction in the northern and southern hemispheres. In Paris, which way does the water drain?

☐ a. Clockwise
☐ b. Counterclockwise

6. Any Parisian can, under certain conditions, join the Association of Winegrowers of Paris. What are the required conditions?

☐ a. To have at least one vine and live within Paris
☐ b. To successfully pass an enology exam
☐ c. To prove ownership of a wine cellar anywhere in France, even if the candidate lives in Paris

7. To what 19th century writer do we owe the novel entitled *Paris in the 20th Century*?

☐ a. Honoré de Balzac
☐ b. Jules Verne
☐ c. Alexandre Dumas

8. Who was the Nicolas de Blégny (1652-1722) who gave his name to a house in the 11th arrondissement?

☐ a. A tactless apothecary
☐ b. A crooked notary
☐ c. A spy on the King's payroll

9. A flea market used to be held at the crossroads of the rue du Faubourg-Saint-Antoine and the avenue Ledru-Rollin. What was sold there?

☐ a. Furniture
☐ b. Scrap metal
☐ c. Rejected meat

10. What curiosity can be seen on the interior of the église Sainte-Marguerite, on rue de la Roquette?

☐ a. A chapel painted entirely as a trompe-l'oeil
☐ b. A group of contemporary stained glass windows
☐ c. A wax statue of a reclining Saint Marguerite

11. What is above the café du 66, on the boulevard Richard-Lenoir?

☐ a. A giant bottle
☐ b. A salvaged marquee from the Guimard metro, put back up at the café
☐ c. A scale model of a dirigible

12. Which of these figures lived in a small bourgeois apartment at 132 boulevard Richard-Lenoir?

☐ a. The illusionist Harry Houdini
☐ b. The serial killer Landru
☐ c. Commissaire Maigret

13. At the intersection of rue de la Roquette and rue de la Croix-Faubin, you might notice five paving stones set in the asphalt. What are they?

☐ a. Vestiges of Thiers's fortifications
☐ b. Foundation slabs which supported the guillotine
☐ c. Stones from the north tower of the old Bastille prison

14. What was built inside a workshop on the rue Titon?

☐ a. The carriage of Louis XVI (that the royal family used in its attempted flight)
☐ b. Pilâtre de Rozier's hot air balloon
☐ c. Bartholdi's Statue of Liberty

15. What did citizen Hébert demand, in the name of the principle of equality, in November 1793?

☐ a. The standardization of clothing for both sexes
☐ b. That all new houses be built with an equal number of floors and chimneys
☐ c. The demolition of all steeples, so that all roofs would be of an equal height

16. The colonnes Morris, columns dedicated to the advertisement of cultural events, made their appearance on Paris's sidewalks around the year 1868, on the initiative of Seine prefect Haussmann. What was his reasoning?

   ☐ a. He didn't want publicity posters stuck on new apartment buildings

   ☐ b. He saw them as a good way to liven up the sidewalks

   ☐ c. It was his response to the demands of theatre directors

17. Of what was "Prosper, Yop la Boum...darling of all the ladies" the king, in the Géo Koger song of 1935?

   ☐ a. Of the pavement

   ☐ b. Of fuss

   ☐ c. Of gingerbread

18. Who invented Monopoly, in 1933?

   ☐ a. A Parisian, of course!

   ☐ b. An American, curiously

   ☐ c. An Auvergnat

19. The Paris of old was filled with minor professions that have since disappeared. Among these were artisans who removed the intestines of animals in order to make strings for musical instruments and tennis rackets. What were these salvagers called?

   ☐ a. Intestineurs

   ☐ b. Tord-boyaux ("Gut twisters")

   ☐ c. Boyautiers ("Gutters")

20. Which metro line serves the greatest number of stations?

☐ a. Line 8
☐ b. Line 9
☐ c. Line 13

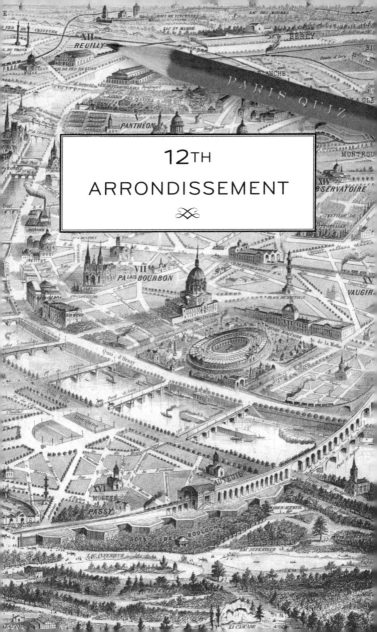

12TH
ARRONDISSEMENT

1. **A monumental animal sculpture adorns the center of the square Saint-Éloi fountain. What animal does it depict?**

   ☐ a. An elephant
   ☐ b. A mammoth
   ☐ c. A whale

2. **The rue Taine bares the name of a philosopher (1828–1893) to whom we owe which thought:**

   ☐ a. "Paris, the farthest point from Paradise, remains nonetheless the only place where it does one good to despair."
   ☐ b. "The way to bore oneself is to know where you're going and how you're getting there."
   ☐ c. "People always talk about the boulevard des Filles-du-Calvaire, but never of the martyrdom of the girls of the boulevard."

3. **What king founded the Quinze-Vingts hospital?**

   ☐ a. Saint Louis
   ☐ b. Louis XIV
   ☐ c. Louis-Philippe

4. **What cities were linked by the mythic Blue Train, a luxurious express whose memory is perpetuated by a gare de Lyon restaurant?**

   ☐ a. Paris and Venice
   ☐ b. Paris and Vladivostok
   ☐ c. Paris and Ventimiglia

5. **What name did the railroad line that linked Paris to Marseille, via Lyon, bear at the end of the 20th century?**

   ☐ a. The Southern Way
   ☐ b. The Imperial Line
   ☐ c. The Provence Express

6. **What Luc Besson film contains a scene shot in the gare de Lyon's Le Train Bleu (Blue Train) restaurant?**

   ☐ a. *The Big Blue*
   ☐ b. *Nikita*
   ☐ c. *Subway*

7. **What archeological relics were uncovered during the refitting of the Ministry of Finances in 1991?**

   ☐ a. The remains of Paleolithic dwellings
   ☐ b. Neolithic canoes
   ☐ c. Merovingian sarcophagi

8. **What is the parc de Bercy's "canyonaustrate"?**

   ☐ a. A 10m-high robot
   ☐ b. A waterfall
   ☐ c. A multiplex cinema

9. **Why is the more than 1,000-year-old Foire du Trône (The Throne Fair) known by that name?**

☐ a. Because the kings of France consistently came to inaugurate the popular festival

☐ b. Because it used to be held at the place du Trône

☐ c. Because the first mechanical attraction there was a spectacular flying throne

10. **What unusual building stands at the edge of the bois de Vincennes, near the lac Daumesnil?**

☐ a. A Tibetan temple
☐ b. An African hut
☐ c. A blue mosque

11. **What metro station name was born of the improbable union of the names of a governor of Senegal and a worker from Lorraine?**

☐ a. Reuilly-Diderot
☐ b. Ledru-Rollin
☐ c. Faidherbe-Chaligny

12. **What racing event is the Paris-Vincennes racetrack known for?**

☐ a. The trot
☐ b. The gallop
☐ c. The obstacle

13. Until 1962, the entrance to the Bastille metro station was decorated with a kiosk built by Guimard, the shape of which evoked...

   ☐ a. A frog
   ☐ b. A dragonfly
   ☐ c. A pagoda

14. What "first" had for its stage the Nation metro station, in 1968?

   ☐ a. The first publicity poster campaign for a non-food product
   ☐ b. The first test of automatic entrance turnstiles
   ☐ c. The first metro-RER connection

15. The group of sculpted figures adorning the center of the place de la Nation is entitled *The Triumph of the Republic*. What is the feminine figure symbolizing the republic perched on?

   ☐ a. A throne
   ☐ b. A globe
   ☐ c. An arc de triomphe

16. What is the width of the narrowest Parisian way?

   ☐ a. 0.35 m
   ☐ b. 0.87 m
   ☐ c. 1.15 m

17. What does the marble plaque affixed to the wall of 304 rue de Charenton say, essentially?

   ☐ a. Edge of Paris — no construction hereafter
   ☐ b. No spitting or urinating
   ☐ c. Building off-limits to collectors, beggars and peddlers

18. Before being relocated to Bercy, the Minister of Finances was housed in a wing of the Louvre. Which?

   ☐ a. The Sully wing
   ☐ b. The Denon wing
   ☐ c. The Richelieu wing

19. Where does the name Picpus, used by a road, a boulevard and a cemetery, come from?

   ☐ a. From a property owner whose land the road goes through
   ☐ b. From an epidemic of itch
   ☐ c. From a train company that had its headquarters in the quarter

20. The "Porte Dorée crime" was the talk of the town in 1937. On Sunday, May 16, a young woman was found mysteriously killed in the metro. Her murderer was never arrested. What was the name of the victim?

   ☐ a. Yvette Chambige
   ☐ b. Mélanie Scheffer
   ☐ c. Laetitia Toureaux

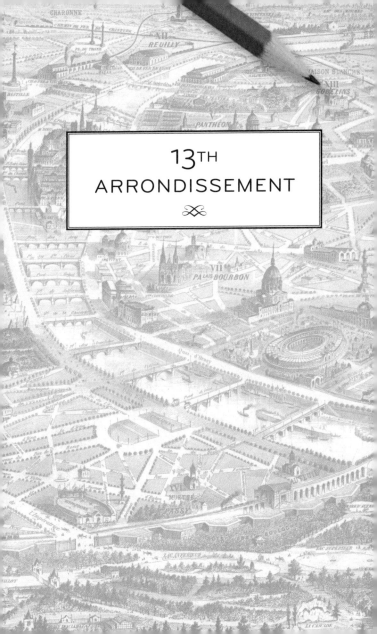

13TH
ARRONDISSEMENT
~~~~~

1. What does the speech bubble accompanying the street sign of the rue René-Goscinny, on the corner of the quai Panhard-et-Levassor, say?

    ☐ a. "They're crazy, these Romans!"
    ☐ b. "By Toutatis!"
    ☐ c. "A bit of magic potion?"

2. In the François Mitterand National Library of France, where are the books stocked?

    ☐ a. In the underground portion, sheltered from light
    ☐ b. In the glass towers, kept from humidity
    ☐ c. In the reading rooms, around the garden

3. How do books kept at the François Mitterand Library circulate from one tower to the other?

    ☐ a. On a conveyor belt
    ☐ b. Propelled by compressed air in a network of PVC tubes
    ☐ c. Transported in carriers that glide on rails affixed to the ceiling

4. In what year was Bièvre river totally covered?

    ☐ a. 1912
    ☐ b. 1937
    ☐ c. 1954

5. What business, known under the name "manufacture des Gobelins," did Jehan Gobelin install along the Bièvre in 1443?

   ☐ a. A textile mill
   ☐ b. A weaving workshop
   ☐ c. A dyeworks

6. In 1662, for the first time, a transportation company offered carriages on a fixed itinerary, at regular hours, for a single price. Who originated this revolution?

   ☐ a. Blaise Pascal
   ☐ b. Voltaire
   ☐ c. Corneille

7. What is the specialty of the Marguerite Durand library?

   ☐ a. Genealogy
   ☐ b. Feminism
   ☐ c. Nordic literature

8. What school, founded in 1889, trains future workers in the bookmaking industry (model makers, graphic artists, photo setters, etc.) by partnering the professional worlds of editing and printing?

   ☐ a. The école Estienne
   ☐ b. The école Boulle
   ☐ c. The école des Chartes

9. **What did the popular expression "to be married to the government of the 13th" mean, as used in the 18th and 19th centuries?**

    ☐ a. To be a lout, a regular of the La Santé Prison (in the 13th arrondissement)
    ☐ b. To be married to a rich widow
    ☐ c. To live with a member of the opposite sex outside of marriage

10. **Who was Corvisart to Napoleon I?**

    ☐ a. His favorite architect
    ☐ b. The commanding general of his armies
    ☐ c. His personal physician

11. **The name of the Chevaleret metro station refers to an object in use in the 18th century. What was it?**

    ☐ a. A light piece of armor protecting the torsos of soldiers
    ☐ b. A weaving loom
    ☐ c. A tool used by tanners

12. **What does the name Tolbiac evoke?**

    ☐ a. A victory
    ☐ b. A pigment prized by dyers
    ☐ c. An ancient convent

13. **What name did the gare d'Austerlitz bear until 1930?**

    ☐ a. Gare d'Orléans
    ☐ b. Gare d'Italie
    ☐ c. Gare Centrale

14. Logically, the gare d'Austerlitz should now be called the "Gare de Slavkov," as the city of Austerlitz has adopted this new name since the time when history made it famous. In what country can it be found today?

   ☐ a. In Russia
   ☐ b. In the Czech Republic
   ☐ c. In Austria

15. What is the longest of the 37 bridges, viaducts and footbridges in Paris?

   ☐ a. The pont Charles-de-Gaulle
   ☐ b. The pont Masséna
   ☐ c. The pont National

16. Who was the Charléty whose name is borne by a Parisian stadium?

   ☐ a. A champion of the 100-meter hurdles
   ☐ b. A mayor of Paris
   ☐ c. A university rector

17. Who is the author of the detective novel *Brouillard au pont de Tolbiac* (Fog on the Tolbiac Bridge)?

   ☐ a. Léo Malet
   ☐ b. Gaston Leroux
   ☐ c. Albert Simonin

18. **What film recounts the true story of a spectacular escape attempt from La Santé Prison?**

    ☐ a. *La Grande Évasion* (The Great Escape)
    ☐ b. *Le Trou* (The Hole)
    ☐ c. *La Belle* (The Deciding Game)

19. **What is peculiar about the rue du Disque?**

    ☐ a. It's an underground road
    ☐ b. It's circular
    ☐ c. It houses the Museum of the Microgroove, at number 3

20. **Who is the architect of the François Mitterand National Library of France?**

    ☐ a. Paul Chemetov
    ☐ b. Dominique Perrault
    ☐ c. Christian de Portzamparc

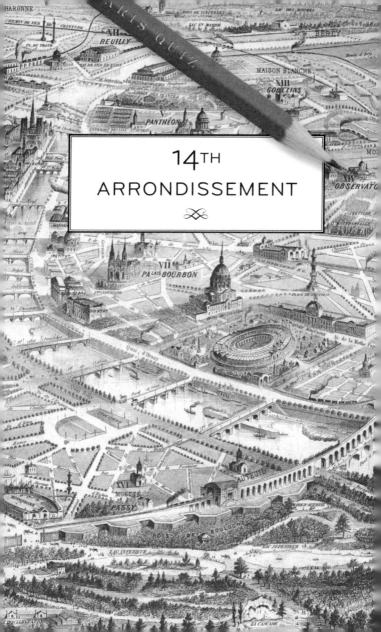

14TH

ARRONDISSEMENT

❧

1. Why does the rue Émile-Richard, which runs a respectable 382 m, include only one street number?

    ☐ a. Because it crosses a cemetery
    ☐ b. Because it runs along a railroad track
    ☐ c. Because it borders the bleak walls of a prison

2. In Greek mythology, who lived on Mount Parnassus (the namesake of Montparnasse)?

    ☐ a. Hermes, the messenger god
    ☐ b. Apollo and the nine muses
    ☐ c. Artemis, goddess of the hunt

3. On October 22, 1895, a train coming from Granville continued onward after arriving at the gare Montparnasse. It crossed the waiting area, burst through the station's façade and fell into the road, cars and passengers in tow. How many victims did it claim?

    ☐ a. Only one
    ☐ b. 36
    ☐ c. 108 (including passengers and persons present in the station's main hall)

4. What is the length of the triple-wide moving walkway of the Montparnasse metro station?

    ☐ a. 185 m
    ☐ b. 235 m
    ☐ c. 350 m

5. **How many stories is the Montparnasse Tower?**

☐ a. 48
☐ b. 59
☐ c. 64

6. **For what reason was a certain Alain Robert questioned by the police on January 17, 1995, at the Montparnasse Tower?**

☐ a. He had climbed the tower
☐ b. He had parachuted off it
☐ c. He had landed his helicopter on the roof

7. **In the Montparnasse cemetery, the shocking grave of M. and Mme. Pigeon never goes unnoticed! It is surmounted by a life-sized bronze sculpture of a scene from the conjugal life of the honorable bourgeois couple. What is the scene?**

☐ a. The spouses are in their bathroom: Madame powders herself at her dressing table while Monsieur shaves, in his shirtsleeves, above the sink
☐ b. The spouses are lying side by side in their king-sized bed: Madame sleeps while Monsieur balances the books
☐ c. The spouses are in their living room: Madame mends clothing while Monsieur, in his robe, smokes a pipe in his armchair

8. **What is unique about the Notre-Dame-du-Travail church, erected in 1900?**

   ☐ a. Its metallic architecture
   ☐ b. It houses a metro entrance under its doorway
   ☐ c. It was originally the Swedish pavilion at the 1889 World's Fair

9. **In the Montparnasse cemetery, what poet originally enjoyed the privilege of having two posthumous residences?**

   ☐ a. Charles Baudelaire
   ☐ b. Arthur Rimbaud
   ☐ c. Paul Verlaine

10. **On November 30th 1779 a certain Philibert Aspairt, searching for the abandoned spirits cellar of Carthusian monks, got lost in the catacombs. How much time went by before he was found?**

   ☐ a. He spent seven days in the dark before rescuers found him at the back of a tunnel, dehydrated but unharmed
   ☐ b. He was found dead three months after his escapade
   ☐ c. His skeleton wasn't discovered until 11 years later

11. **What guided visitors through the catacombs until 1972, when the installation of electricity ended candlelit visits?**

    ☐ a. A black line painted on the ceiling of the tunnels
    ☐ b. White stones sealed into the ground
    ☐ c. Ropes running along the walls

12. **What is the ratio of remains contained in the catacombs to current habitants of Paris?**

    ☐ a. There are three times as many skeletons as living Parisians
    ☐ b. There are as many Parisians on the earth as under it
    ☐ c. There are three times fewer skeletons than flesh-and-blood Parisians

13. **What is the curious "barrel" that can be seen during a visit to the catacombs?**

    ☐ a. A circular piece of stone that served to block the entrances to tunnels
    ☐ b. An actual wooden barrel collecting seepage water, used as a fountain by workers
    ☐ c. A thick pillar covered in skulls and tibias

14. **Why did fountain workers once raise trout in the Montsouris water reservoir, built in 1874 by the engineer Belgrand?**

    ☐ a. To liven up their daily snack with delicious fried fish
    ☐ b. To monitor water quality
    ☐ c. To respect tradition, the trout being the symbol of the fountain workers' guild

15. **Why did the entrepreneur who presided over the construction of the Montsouris park's artificial lake commit suicide after its opening, in 1878?**

☐ a. The lake was completely dry on the day of its opening

☐ b. He had forgotten to stock the lake with fish and swans

☐ c. The public vehemently criticized the shape chosen for the body of water

16. **The name Montsouris comes from a corruption of "Moque-Souris" (Mock-Mouse). Why did the quarter have this nickname?**

☐ a. It had been divided into plots by Messieurs Moque and Souris

☐ b. It was full of abandoned windmills invaded by rodents

☐ c. It was notoriously frequented by women of little virtue (called "mice"), who abused the unfortunates that fell into their nets

17. **What is the name of the Ricardo Bofill sculpture-fountain, which occupies the center of the place de Catalogne?**

☐ a. *The Discobolus*

☐ b. *The Liquid Arena*

☐ c. *The Crucible of Time*

18. What can be found in the basement of the Paris Observatory?

☐ a. Foucault's pendulum
☐ b. A talking clock
☐ c. A standard meter

19. What is peculiar about the architecture of the Paris Observatory?

☐ a. The walls of its laboratories are perfectly round, without interruption
☐ b. Iron and wood were shunned during its construction
☐ c. It rests on oil-filled caissons so that earthquakes don't skew scientific readings

20. What is the name of the train line, realized under Louis-Philippe, linking the Chevreuse valley to the Denfert-Rochereau station?

☐ a. The Orléans way
☐ b. The Sceaux line
☐ c. The green stream

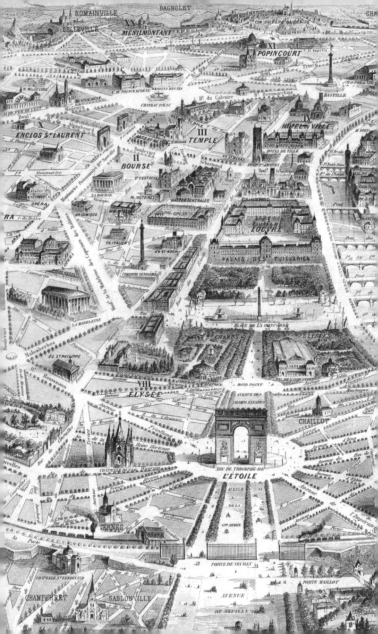

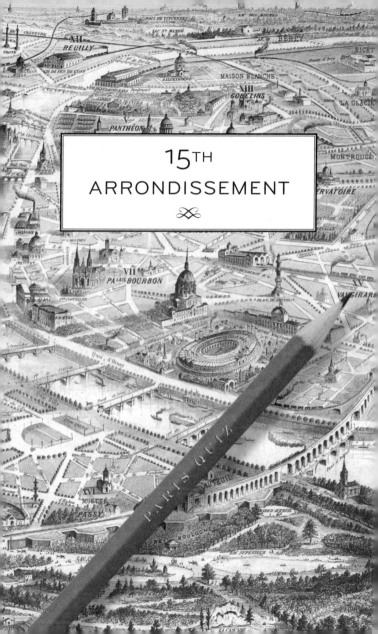

15TH
ARRONDISSEMENT

〰

1. Like all of Paris's arrondissements, the 15th consists of four quarters, which are: Necker, Grenelle, Javel and...

   ☐ a. Saint-Lambert
   ☐ b. Sainte-Marguerite
   ☐ c. Saint-Victor

2. How does the église Sainte-Rita distinguish itself from the rest of Paris's catholic churches?

   ☐ a. It attracts all kinds of lost souls, who come to pray to the patron saint of desperate cases
   ☐ b. The mass is said in Latin, according to the rite of Pius V
   ☐ c. Once a year it welcomes animals for a collective blessing

3. The sculptor Bourdelle has his museum, unsurprisingly, on the rue Antoine-Bourdelle. More surprising is the fact that this artist had people call him Antoine, even though his parents baptized him Émile. Why?

   ☐ a. Out of admiration for Antoine Rodin, who he considered his teacher
   ☐ b. Because he hated the nickname Mimile
   ☐ c. Because his wife's name was Cléopâtre

4. At 91 rue Lecourbe a miniscule Russian church, complete with onion dome, is hidden at the rear of a backyard. What natural wonder is found inside this place of worship?

☐ a. A tree trunk, planted in the ground, that shoots through the roof of the church

☐ b. A trodden-earth floor, to "elevate the soul while keeping the feet on the ground"

☐ c. Interior walls covered in ivy

5. 36 rue des Morillons is where found objects (or lost ones, depending on how you look at it) end up. What is the origin of the street's namesake, a "morillon"?

☐ a. A type of grape

☐ b. A monastery

☐ c. A mushroom

6. In the Georges-Brassens park there are two most peculiar gardens. One allows the blind to experience the joys of botany thanks to signs in braille. The other is...

☐ a. A garden and hands-on museum where one can touch sculptures

☐ b. An aromatic garden where a thousand and one smells drift

☐ c. A gourmand's garden, stocked only with edible plants and flowers

7. What is the purpose of "The Beehive," located since 1902 in the passage de Dantzig?

    ☐ a. The production of wild honey
    ☐ b. The protection of the environment
    ☐ c. The welcoming of artists

8. Who was Boucicaut, whose name is borne by a hospital, a square, a street and a metro station?

    ☐ a. The owner of the land on which the porte de Versailles exhibition ground was built
    ☐ b. The founder of Le Bon Marché
    ☐ c. The engineer who coordinated work on the western train line

9. In the northeast part of the parc André-Citroën, six small greenhouses echo six themed gardens, situated below. Each of the gardens has a color, symbolically associated with...

    ☐ a. A metal
    ☐ b. A planet
    ☐ c. A day of the week

10. Bleach, known in French as "eau de Javel," was born on the banks of the Seine at the end of the 18th century. Why was it given the name "eau de Javel"?

☐ a. Its inventor was named Augustin Javel
☐ b. The first factory was built in the village of Javel
☐ c. Just as butchers speak "louchebem" (a slang based on transforming words), washerwomen transformed words by shifting the first consonant to the end of the word and replacing it with a j (thus the word "lave," wash, becomes "javel")

11. What metro station was called Beaugrenelle until 1945?

☐ a. Charles-Michels
☐ b. Javel
☐ c. Avenue-Émile-Zola

12. What pops up at the bend at 69 rue Castagnary?

☐ a. A Basque pelota wall
☐ b. A Breton lighthouse
☐ c. A Savoyard chalet

13. Who was Falguière?

☐ a. A sculptor
☐ b. A physicist
☐ c. A general

14. **What contemporary artist is the creator of *l'Oiseau lunaire*, a 2 m-high bronze sculpture placed in the center of the square Blomet?**

   ☐ a. Paul Landowski
   ☐ b. Joan Miró
   ☐ c. François Pompon

15. **Where does the name of the Bir-Hakeim metro station come from?**

   ☐ a. From an Arabic form of address
   ☐ b. From the headgear worn by French colonial troops
   ☐ c. From an oasis in the middle of the Libyan desert

16. **Who lived "Alone with mommy, in a very old apartment, on rue Sarasate"?**

   ☐ a. Charles Aznavour
   ☐ b. Gilbert Bécaud
   ☐ c. Yves Montaud

17. **What is the scale of the replica of the Statue of Liberty that stands at the tip of the Île aux Cygnes?**

   ☐ a. 1/2
   ☐ b. 1/5
   ☐ c. 1/10

18. **What happened to the Île aux Cygnes' Statue of Liberty in 1937?**

    ☐ a. It was dressed in a starred red, white and blue outfit, a nod to the American flag
    ☐ b. An electrical system was hooked up to the top of the flame, making it a glimmering torch
    ☐ c. It was turned around on its pedestal

19. **For how long are found objects kept by the lost and found service on the rue des Morillons?**

    ☐ a. 4 months
    ☐ b. A year and a day
    ☐ c. A year and a half

20. **Under whose patronage is the rue de la Convention church (near the quai Andé-Citroën and the port de Javel) placed?**

    ☐ a. Saint Christopher, patron of voyagers
    ☐ b. Saint John the Baptist, patron of leatherworkers
    ☐ c. Saint Veronica, patron of laundry women

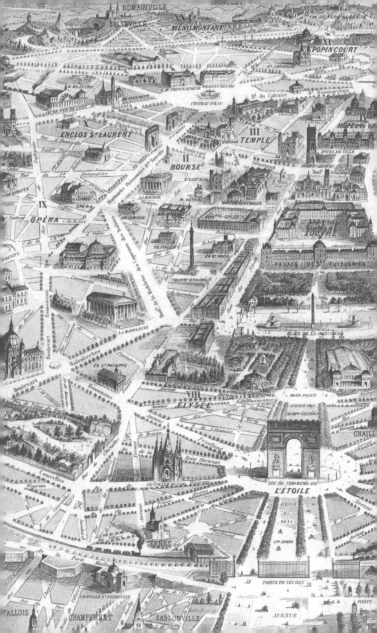

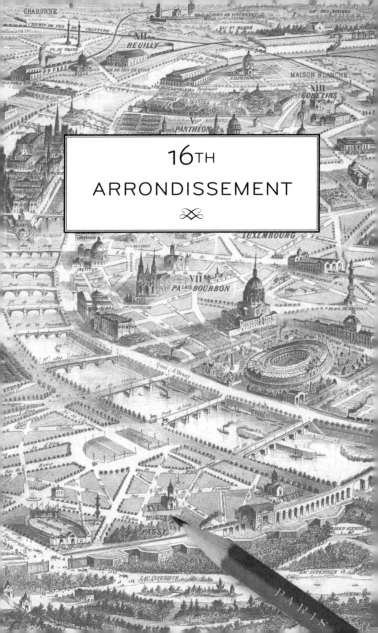

16TH
ARRONDISSEMENT

❧

1. **How many lakes can the bois de Boulogne boast?**

    ☐ a. 1
    ☐ b. 2
    ☐ c. 3

2. **In what year was a gilded bronze flame placed in the place de l'Alma?**

    ☐ a. 1934, on the occasion of the 50th anniversary of the Statue of Liberty
    ☐ b. 1987, for the centenary of the *International Herald Tribune*
    ☐ c. 1998, one year exactly after the accident in the tunnel that cut short the life of Princess Diana

3. **What memory does the word Trocadéro evoke?**

    ☐ a. The taking of an Andalusian fort
    ☐ b. A battle won by Napoleon's army in a Piedmontese valley
    ☐ c. The name of the architect who built the palace (since demolished) for the 1878 World's Fair

4. **Where do the virtuosos of Roller Team 340 hold court?**

    ☐ a. On the esplanade of the Eiffel Tower
    ☐ b. At the Trocadéro
    ☐ c. On the quai Branly (by the pont d'Iéna)

5. **What is the fountain with jets in the Trocadéro gardens called?**

   ☐ a. The Rights of Man Fountain
   ☐ b. The Warsaw Fountain
   ☐ c. The Polypore Fountain (after the species of mushroom)

6. **What museum has the address 16 rue de la Faisanderie?**

   ☐ a. The Clemenceau Museum
   ☐ b. The Museum of Counterfeiting
   ☐ c. The Baccarat Museum

7. **Who was Roland Garros?**

   ☐ a. A tennis player
   ☐ b. A philanthropist banker
   ☐ c. An aviator

8. **What is unique about the water that flows from the square Lamartine fountain, in Passy?**

   ☐ a. It has a temperature of 25°C
   ☐ b. It is rich in iron and mineral salts
   ☐ c. It's sulfuric

9. **What museum can one visit on the rue des Eaux?**

   ☐ a. The Museum of Robots
   ☐ b. The Wine Museum
   ☐ c. The Museum of Counterfeiting

10. **What 624-square-meter painting occupies a whole room of The Museum of Modern Art of the City of Paris?**

    ☐ a. Claude Monet's *Water Lillies*
    ☐ b. Henri Matisse's *The Danse*
    ☐ c. Raoul Dufy's *The Electric Fairy*

11. **Who does the bois de Boulogne belong to?**

    ☐ a. The French state
    ☐ b. The city of Paris
    ☐ c. Wealthy residents

12. **What is the motto of the Maison de la Radio?**

    ☐ a. "A radio in every house, everywhere in France."
    ☐ b. "Friend of sound and enemy of noise."
    ☐ c. "May music accompany you."

13. **What country is particularly favored in the place names of the 16th arrondissement?**

    ☐ a. Italy
    ☐ b. The United States
    ☐ c. Brazil

14. **What fable is acted out at the feet of the statue of La Fontaine that decorates the Ranelagh garden?**

    ☐ a. *The Ant and the Grasshopper*
    ☐ b. *The Tortoise and the Hare*
    ☐ c. *The Fox and the Crow*

15. Who was the Kléber who left his name to a metro station?

☐ a. A rich art collector
☐ b. An Alsatian general
☐ c. A tire manufacturer

16. What does the name of the Boissière metro station evoke?

☐ a. An old religious rite
☐ b. The existence of a forest
☐ c. The presence of an important sawmill

17. Who founded the Guimet museum?

☐ a. An industrialist from Lyon
☐ b. A Corsican naturalist
☐ c. An explorer from Nantes

18. What gate of Paris evokes an old hunting pavilion, transformed into a small chateau in the 16th century, rebuilt by Gabriel in the 18th century and demolished in the 1920s?

☐ a. The porte Saint-Cloud
☐ b. The porte Molitor
☐ c. The porte de la Muette

19. **The name of the Léna metro station recalls a Napoleonic victory over the Prussians in 1806. In what country can the town of Léna be found?**

☐ a. In Germany
☐ b. In Russia
☐ c. In Austria

20. **What is the specialty of the Dapper museum?**

☐ a. The story of the automobile
☐ b. African art
☐ c. The history of dentistry

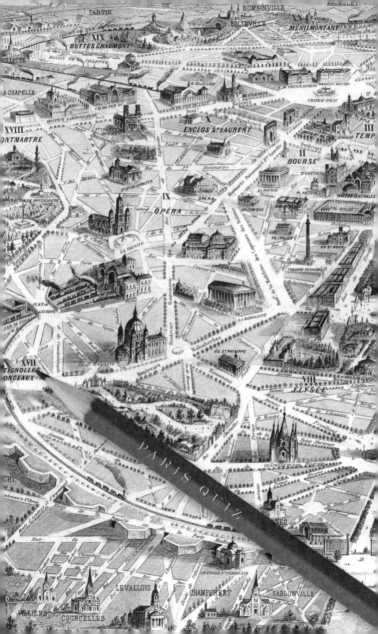

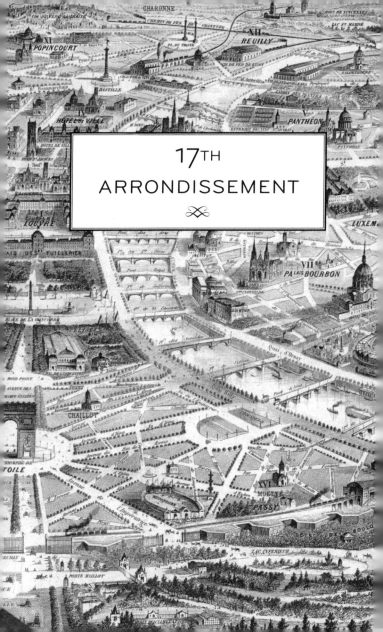

17TH

ARRONDISSEMENT

❧

1. It was in the workshop of a plumber at 25 rue de Chazelles that the sculptor Bartholdi assembled his Statue of Liberty. What woman's face did he first use as a model?

   ☐ a. His mother's
   ☐ b. His mistress's
   ☐ c. Sarah Bernhardt's

2. What was the Argentine metro station called prior to 1948?

   ☐ a. Río de la Plata
   ☐ b. Obligado
   ☐ c. There was no station at the location before 1948

3. What was the profession of the Pereire brothers, whose name was given to a boulevard in 1853, during their lifetimes?

   ☐ a. Aviators
   ☐ b. Bankers
   ☐ c. Mathematicians

4. What do the names of the Villiers, Monceau and Courcelles metro stations recall?

   ☐ a. Old villages and hamlets
   ☐ b. Marshals of the Empire
   ☐ c. Victories of the Napoleonic army

5. There used to be, by the side of the porte des Ternes, an establishment called the "ratodrome," which was frequented, notably, by Raymond Queneau and Jacques Prévert. What activity was practiced there?

☐ a. Rat races
☐ b. Literary debates where the absurd was the order of the day
☐ c. The training of "ratters," dogs that catch rats

6. What is the reason for the incongruous presence of a Byzantine-style chapel between the Boulevard Périphérique (Paris's ring road) and the place du Général-Koenig?

☐ a. A miracle took place on the exact spot
☐ b. A prince was the victim of a carriage accident at the site
☐ c. It is a vestige of the 1889 World's Fair

7. Where did Nana, the Zola heroine, live?

☐ a. The rue de Tocqueville
☐ b. The avenue des Villiers
☐ c. The boulevard Malesherbes

8. On the place du Général-Catroux, the extravagant façade of the hotel Gaillard steals the spotlight from all the other buildings. What institution does it house?

☐ a. A branch of the Banque de France
☐ b. The Jean-Jacques Henner museum
☐ c. An annex to the storerooms of the Louvre

9. The cité des Fleurs is a delightful private street, lined with houses that have gardens, drawn in 1847 through the heart of the Épinettes quarter. What obligation did the first owners have to agree to?

   ☐ a. To name their houses after a cactus or spiny shrub

   ☐ b. To plant three flowering trees in their gardens

   ☐ c. To take turns watering the flower beds and communal lawns

10. Why did the aviator Charles Godefroy dive under the Arc de triomphe in his biplane on August 7, 1919?

   ☐ a. To impress his girlfriend

   ☐ b. To express the discontent of French aviators

   ☐ c. Because he was completely drunk

11. The porte Maillot owes its name to a game played at the location under Louis XIV. What was the game?

   ☐ a. Skittles

   ☐ b. A racket game

   ☐ c. Croquet

12. How many avenues open onto the place Charles-de-Gaulle?

   ☐ a. 11

   ☐ b. 12

   ☐ c. 13

13. By what name is the haut-relief *Départ des Volontaires* (*The Departure of the Volunteers*), sculpted by Rude to adorn one side of the Arc de triomphe, better known?

   ☐ a. *La Marseillaise*
   ☐ b. *La Parisienne*
   ☐ c. *L'Arlésienne*

14. What is the official name of the square in which the Arc de triomphe stands?

   ☐ a. Place de l'Étoile
   ☐ b. Place Charles-de-Gaulle
   ☐ c. Rond-point des Champs-Élysées

15. The plaine des Sablons was put to a suprising use in 1786: Parmentier grew potato plants there on a large scale. What trick did he use to get skeptical Parisians to consume the unknown tuber?

   ☐ a. He fenced in the plantation and had it guarded by watchmen to pique public curiosity
   ☐ b. He set up open-air cafés all around the site, where potato-based plates were served for one sou
   ☐ c. He offered a tidy reward to all singers, public entertainers and fairground criers who would praise the potato in their refrains

16. **Why did 19th-century women shun the parties given by M. Cernuschi in his parc Monceau home, despite the grandeur of the events?**

   ☐ a. The host had a reputation for having wandering hands

   ☐ b. They didn't appreciate M. Cernuschi's exotic knickknack collection

   ☐ c. They found that the lighting of the home made them look bad

17. **Paris's first erotic theatre opened in 1862 on the rue de la Santé (currently the rue de Saussure). Who were the protagonists playing on the stages there?**

   ☐ a. Mannequins carved out of wood

   ☐ b. Silhouettes made by shadow puppets

   ☐ c. Comedians short on gigs

18. **In the 19th century, what profession did a "bagotier" practice?**

   ☐ a. He ran behind taxis, in order to help travelers carry their baggage once they arrived at their destination

   ☐ b. He attracted clients into a store or a fair stand with his silver tongue

   ☐ c. He manufactured rings, signet rings and watch chains

19. **What 19th-century invention increased the value of the high floors in apartment buildings?**

☐ a. The bow window
☐ b. The elevator
☐ c. Running water

20. **In the 18th century, what was the intention of someone taking a "carabas," a "coucou" or a "chamber pot"?**

☐ a. To travel
☐ b. To relieve themselves
☐ c. To quench their thirst

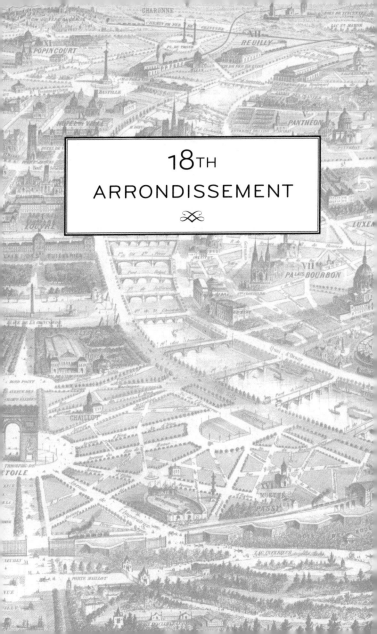

18TH
ARRONDISSEMENT
∞

1. What artist is the creator of the curious *Passe-Muraille*, a sculpture that seems to emerge from one of the walls of the place Marcel-Aymé?

   ☐ a. César
   ☐ b. Jean Marais
   ☐ c. Jean Dubuffet

2. Where does the name of the Goutte-d'Or ("Taste of Gold") quarter come from?

   ☐ a. In the middle ages, vineyards produced a renowned nectar there
   ☐ b. Until the 20th century the quarter, devoid of natural resources, was supplied by porters who sold their water at prices that constituted a small fortune
   ☐ c. It owes the nickname to the numerous sellers of oriental jewels that could be found there

3. What is unique about the rue Cavallotti?

   ☐ a. All of its building fronts have preserved their medieval timbering
   ☐ b. The iron roller shutters on all the shops are painted with reproductions of famous paintings
   ☐ c. It's equipped with speakers that play opera tunes in a loop

4. The rue du Chevalier-de-La-Barre bears the name of a young man tortured to death in 1766, at the age of 19. What crime earned him this punishment?

    a. He deserted from his regiment

    b. He failed to salute a religious procession

    c. He seduced a Carmelite nun

5. What ornament can the picturesque rue du Chevalier-de-La-Barre, which climbs the Montmartre hill, boast?

  ☐ a. A lighting system that draws a shower of stars on the pavement

  ☐ b. A musical kiosk animated with figurines

  ☐ c. Avant-gardist streetlights by Philippe Starck

6. What characterizes the Abbesses metro station?

  ☐ a. It is the deepest of Paris's 297 stations

  ☐ b. Its two platforms are staggered by approximately ten meters due to the slope of the Montmartre hill

  ☐ c. It's only open on weekends and holidays

7. Why is the stone of the Sacré-Coeur Basilica still so white, in spite of pollution and bad weather?

  ☐ a. Because it is cleaned every week

  ☐ b. Because the height of the hill puts it outside of the range of exhaust fumes

  ☐ c. Because the limestone from which it is made whitens with even the slightest rain

8. What is the name of the nearly 19-ton bell hanging in the bell tower of the Sacré-Coeur Basilica?

    ☐ a. The Auvergnate
    ☐ b. The Berrichonne
    ☐ c. The Savoyarde

9. How is the Saint-Vincent garden, on the Montmartre hill, different from other green spaces?

    ☐ a. It's a mineral garden
    ☐ b. It's a wild garden
    ☐ c. It's a vineyard

10. To what divinity was the temple standing on the Montmartre hill, then isolated from the city, dedicated in Gallo-Roman times?

    ☐ a. Mercury
    ☐ b. Jupiter
    ☐ c. Mars

11. What poet, a familiar figure in the cité Véron, wrote the following verse: "A child of the third, I lived on the fourth in a house from the nineteenth"?

    ☐ a. Jacques Prévert
    ☐ b. Boris Vian
    ☐ c. Robert Desnos

12. When did the hill of Montmartre first go back to its wine-producing past by replanting vines on its slopes?

    ☐ a. 1933
    ☐ b. 1955
    ☐ c. 1978

13. In 1893, *Yvette's Bedtime* was highly applauded by the audience of the Divan japonais, a Montmartre cabaret. What type of show was the innovative spectacle?

☐ a. A performance of marionettes dressed in goat skin, made by the patients of the Pitié-Salpêtrière asylum

☐ b. The first strip tease

☐ c. The first film projection

14. Where does the name of the store Tati, founded by Jules Ouaki in 1948, come from?

☐ a. The young Jules had been raised by his aunt, his dear Tati, whose memory he honored with the store

☐ b. It's an homage to his mother, whose first name was Tita, in slang

☐ c. It's an acronym for the slogan the store used on opening: "Tout s'Achète et se Trouve ici" ("Everything can be bought, and can be found here")

15. Of the 13 windmills that stood on the Montmartre hill at the end of the 18th century, how many are left today?

☐ a. Unfortunately, none

☐ b. Only two

☐ c. There are still six

16. Why did François Truffaut demand to be buried in the cimetière de Montmartre?

   ☐ a. It was the only Parisian cemetery that granted him an authorization to shoot there
   ☐ b. The site was, on the contrary, denied to one of his films
   ☐ c. The Truffaut family vault is there

17. What rue des Saules cabaret was successively called "The Thieves' Rendezvous," "The Assassins' Cabaret," and then "My Countryside," before adopting its current name?

   ☐ a. The Divan Japonais
   ☐ b. The Caveau de la Butte
   ☐ c. The Lapin Agile

18. Since 1963, the titles of all the revues at the Moulin Rouge have started with the same letter of the alphabet. Which?

   ☐ a. F
   ☐ b. M
   ☐ c. S

19. To what painter do we owe the painting titled *Le Moulin de la Galette* (1876)?

   ☐ a. Édouard Manet
   ☐ b. Auguste Renoir
   ☐ c. Henri de Toulouse-Lautrec

20. **What was the name of the windmill demolished in 1912 to open the avenue Junot?**

☐ a. The Testin Mill
☐ b. The Pepper Mill
☐ c. The Powder Mill

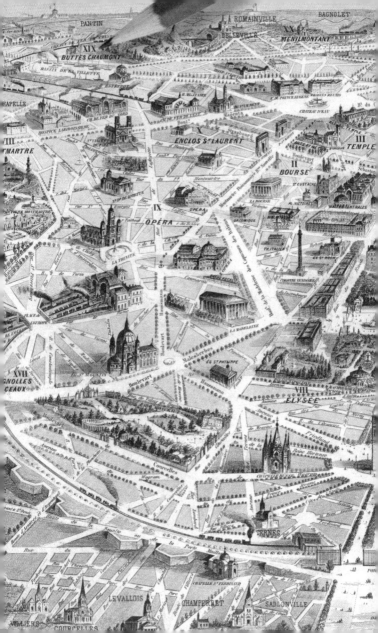

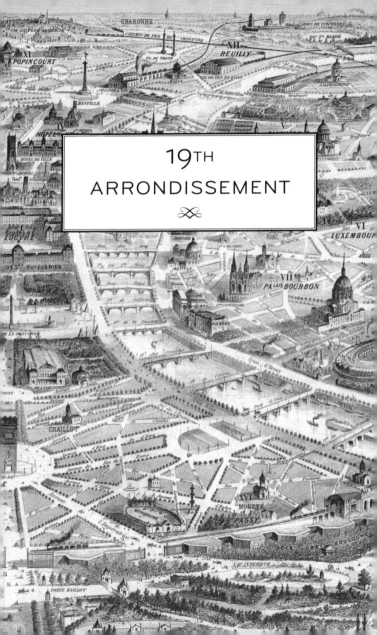

19TH
ARRONDISSEMENT

1. **What Parisian record does the Place-des-Fêtes metro station hold?**

    ☐ a. It's the deepest
    ☐ b. Its platforms are the narrowest
    ☐ c. It possesses the longest escalator

2. **What is the name of the small temple that dominates the parc des Buttes-Chaumont from atop a rock?**

    ☐ a. The Temple of Aphrodite
    ☐ b. The Sibyl's Temple
    ☐ c. The Temple of Galatea

3. **What shape does the green patch in the parc de Buttes-Chaumont form, when seen from a plane?**

    ☐ a. A star
    ☐ b. A heart
    ☐ c. A croissant

4. **What multipurpose auditorium sports a red airplane perched atop a concrete column as a sign?**

    ☐ a. The Zénith de Paris
    ☐ b. The Cité de la musique
    ☐ c. The Grande Halle de La Villette

5. **What is peculiar about the pont de Crimée, which separates La Villette pond from the canal de l'Ourcq?**

    ☐ a. It's a floating bridge
    ☐ b. It's a lift bridge
    ☐ c. It's a swing bridge

6. The date of the opening of La Villette's Cité des sciences et de l'industrie (March 13, 1986) was deliberately chosen to coincide with a great scientific event. What?

☐ a. The launch of the satellite *Spot 2*
☐ b. The appearance of Halley's comet
☐ c. The centennial of the birth of Albert Einstein

7. The name of the place de la Bataille-de-Stalingrad recalls a Soviet victory over German troops in 1943. But there is no longer a Stalingrad in Russia, the city having been rechristened in 1961. What has it been known as since?

☐ a. Leningrad
☐ b. Petrograd
☐ c. Volgograd

8. What was the specialty of the professor Robert Debré (1882–1978), to whom the hospital on the boulevard Sérurier is dedicated?

☐ a. Surgery
☐ b. Pediatrics
☐ c. Research

9. What contemporary artist created the 4 m-high, multicolored plastic character that has livened the terraces of the Robert-Debré Hospital since 1988?

☐ a. Richard Baquié
☐ b. Jean Dubuffet
☐ c. Niki de Saint-Phalle

10. **Why do the houses around the rue de Mouzaïa have only one floor?**

    ☐ a. So as not to be too heavy
    ☐ b. So as not to obstruct the view
    ☐ c. As a reminder that Paris grew by annexing villages

11. **In what station did Claude Monet, after whom a villa in the 19th arrondissement is named, pose his easel on numerous occasions, in order to paint its different aspects?**

    ☐ a. The gare d'Austerlitz
    ☐ b. The gare d'Orsay
    ☐ c. The gare Saint-Lazare

12. **Where is the source of the Seine, after which a quay bordering the La Villette pond is named?**

    ☐ a. On Mount Gerbier-de-Jonc
    ☐ b. On the Langres Plateau
    ☐ c. In the Faucilles Mountains

13. **The rue des Carrières-d'Amérique ("Quarries of America") evokes a time when alabaster was extracted from the ground there. What were the quarries nicknamed?**

    ☐ a. Uncle Sam Quarries
    ☐ b. Mississippi Quarries
    ☐ c. Far West Quarries

14. **What is the length of the perimeter drawn by the Périphérique (Paris's ring road)?**

    ☐ a. 25 km
    ☐ b. 32 km
    ☐ c. 35 km

15. **In the 19th century, what were the men called whose job it was to accompany drunks home?**

    ☐ a. Lazzarones
    ☐ b. Saint-Bernards
    ☐ c. Guardian Angels

16. **The Wall of the Farmers-General was a tax wall where the octroi and taxes on fuel, meat, fruits and vegetables entering or leaving Paris were paid. How many gates did the wall have?**

    ☐ a. 50
    ☐ b. 60
    ☐ c. 70

17. **What civic-minded inscription was printed on metro tickets until the 1940s?**

    ☐ a. "Upon exiting, throw in garbage"
    ☐ b. "Thank you for not spitting on the platforms"
    ☐ c. "It is prohibited to cross the tracks"

18. **When was the term "banlieu" ("suburb") coined?**

    □ a. In the 15th century, with the extension of the city
    □ b. In the 19th century, upon the annexation of the outskirts
    □ c. In the 20th century, with the appearance of new cities

19. **At 161 avenue Jean-Jaurès there is a "cayenne." What is it?**

    □ a. A burnt building whose internal structure is visible
    □ b. A house to welcome "compagnons du Tour de France," young traveling apprentices in a variety of disciplines
    □ c. A well equipped with a semi-mechanical drawing system

20. **In what year did the General Slaughterhouse of Paris leave its La Villette site?**

    □ a. 1970
    □ b. 1974
    □ c. 1978

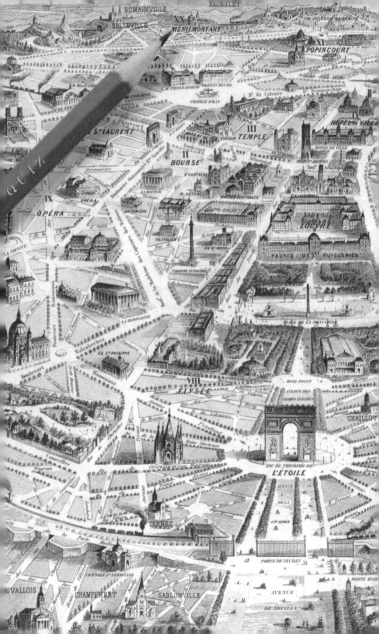

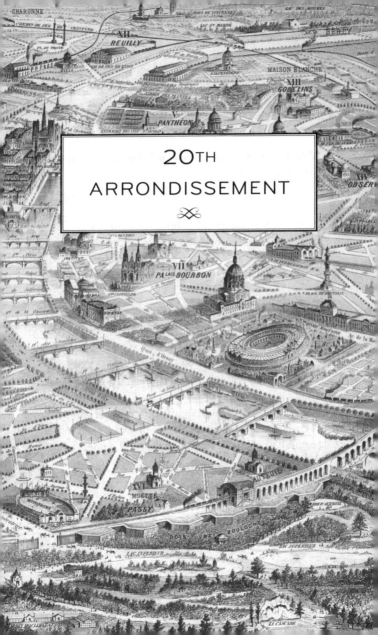

20TH
ARRONDISSEMENT

1. **What is peculiar about the rue Ligner?**

   ☐ a. It forms a perfect line, as straight as an I
   ☐ b. It takes the form of a U
   ☐ c. It snakes like a mountain road

2. **Why does the name of the rue Julien-Lacroix seem somewhat predestined?**

   ☐ a. It cuts through the rue Labannière at a right angle
   ☐ b. A famous brand of bleach neighbors a manufacturer of crucifixes on the road
   ☐ c. It houses a catholic church, a protestant church and a synagogue

3. **What invention did Claude Chappe test on July 12, 1793, on the Belleville Hill, the highest point in Paris?**

   ☐ a. The bicycle brake
   ☐ b. The hot air balloon
   ☐ c. The telegraph

4. **Who is the writer and fan of mathematical games who rests in the Père-Lachaise cemetery in a vault in the form of 32 squares, similar to those of a chessboard?**

   ☐ a. Raymond Queneau
   ☐ b. Georges Perec
   ☐ c. Raymond Roussel

5. **For what reason were the remains of Molière, La Fontaine, and the lovers Abélard and Héloïse transferred with great pomp to the Père-Lachaise cemetery in 1817?**

   ☐ a. The church refused to welcome these sordid characters in a parish cemetery or chapel
   ☐ b. Parisians wanted to see their favorite celebrities resting in the most prestigious of cemeteries
   ☐ c. To promote the new cemetery and attract new "clients"

6. **What type of tree did the poet Alfred de Musset wish to see growing on his tomb in Père-Lachaise?**

   ☐ a. A weeping willow
   ☐ b. A Japanese cherry tree
   ☐ c. A stone pine

7. **What is the address of the Père-Lachaise cemetery?**

   ☐ a. Passage d'Enfer (Hell's Passage)
   ☐ b. Rue de Paradis (Heaven Street)
   ☐ c. Rue du Repos (Resting Street)

8. **What innovation was offered to the users of the Père-Lachaise metro station in 1909?**

   ☐ a. The first escalator
   ☐ b. The first mechanical ticket puncher
   ☐ c. The first automatic entry gate

9. In what Balzac novel does the young Rastignac shout, from the heights of Père-Lachaise: "Paris, it's just the two of us now!"

☐ a. *Old Goriot*
☐ b. *Lost Illustions*
☐ c. *The Magic Skin*

10. In the Père-Lachaise cemetery, the tomb of Oscar Wilde portrays a winged sphinx, endowed with certain virile attributes that can't be ignored. The appendage shocked two British tourists who came to pay tribute to the memory of the writer in 1961. What dramatic action did the ladies take in their prudish alarm?

☐ a. They smashed the scandalously prominent parts with blows from rocks
☐ b. They made a scene in the office of the chief curator of the cemetery
☐ c. They went straight to their embassy to demand direct intervention by the British government

11. A tenacious superstition is attached to the bronze reclining statue of the journalist Victor Noir, in the Père-Lachaise cemetery. What are the alleged powers of the statue?

☐ a. To augment the fertility of wives and find a husband for young ladies
☐ b. To ensure brilliant success on exams
☐ c. To protect against invasive mother-in-laws and jealous spouses

12. **What was the nickname for the Parisian thugs who made the law on the streets of Belleville at the start of the 20th century?**

☐ a. Apaches
☐ b. Redskins
☐ c. Sioux

13. **In the 20th century, archeologists discovered remains dating from the Neolithic period on the heights of Belleville. What animal used to graze in the area?**

☐ a. A mammoth
☐ b. A rhinoceros
☐ c. An aurochs

14. **What are the inhabitants of the Ménilmontant quarter called?**

☐ a. Ménilmontiens
☐ b. Ménilmontants
☐ c. Ménilmontois

15. **Where does the name of the rue des Panoyaux come from?**

☐ a. From a nearby well, in which a number of careless people drowned
☐ b. From a variety of seedless grape cultivated on the site
☐ c. From a maker of signs and notice boards neighboring the road

16. What small-time occupation was practiced, at the beginning of the 20th century, at the gate of the Père-Lachaise cemetery?

☐ a. Dog-sitting
☐ b. The sale of tissues
☐ c. The recitation of prayers on demand

17. What is the gradient of the rue Gasnier-Guy, the steepest in Paris?

☐ a. 9.7%
☐ b. 12.1%
☐ c. 17.4%

18. In the 19th century, what was the favorite motif of the painters Stanislas Lépine and Albert Marquet?

☐ a. The quays and bridges of the Seine
☐ b. The life on the Montmartre hill
☐ c. Boulevards at the end of the day

19. The major east-west road through Paris, lined with arches and monuments, stretches 8 km from the Louvre to the Grande Arche de La Défense. Only one other city in the world has a comparable road. Which?

☐ a. Mexico City
☐ b. Saint Petersburg
☐ c. Beijing

20. To what element is the museum that crowns the parc de Belleville dedicated?

☐ a. Water
☐ b. Air
☐ c. Fire

ANSWERS

❦

1ST ARRONDISSEMENT

✖

1. (b) To Baltard, iron was a vulgar, industrial product, contemptible in comparison to nobler stone. A dedicated civil servant, Baltard nevertheless followed the instructions of Napoleon III: "Iron, nothing but iron!" Ironically, the pavilions of Les Halles brought a great deal of praise to Baltard, who is today considered the pioneer of metal architecture.

2. (a) The Vendôme column was cast with the bronze of 1200 Russian and Austrian cannons taken at Austerlitz. Around the column unravels a relief, depicting 76 scenes from the campaign of 1805, from the departure from camp at Boulogne to the battle of Austerlitz. The scenes are riddled with anachronism: the boats are in the style of Roman warships and the trees of the Danube valley are curiously endowed with the foliage of olive trees.

3. (c) The quatrain makes allusion to a sundial in the jardin du Palais-Royal, much used during the 1750s. It was replaced in 1784 by an acoustic meridian — a miniature cannon that fired each day exactly at solar noon. The device was often stolen and subsequently replaced over the course of the centuries. It is currently visible in the center of the flowerbeds, aligned perfectly with Paris's meridian.

4. (a) Legend has it that the officer's coffee was brought out in a chamber pot.

5. (c) Although the sale of decorations is open (ribbons are sold as well), their wearing is regulated. Thus, a person who hasn't been honored can't wear the Légion d'honneur or the Palmes académiques, except in the intimacy of their own living room.

6. (a) The little red man of the Tuileries appeared only to alert kings to the imminence of their death. He disappeared when the king died.

7. (a) The statue depicts Mariolle, a soldier renowned for his great strength; he was known to do arms drills using a cannon as a rifle. To "faire a Mariolle" means to show off.

8. (c) The pool is octagonal, while its counterpart near the Arc de Triomphe du Carrousel is round.

9. (b) The fontaine des Innocents found itself temporarily perched on a scaffold.

10. (b) The Forts des Halles didn't just unload carts. They also made sure that order was maintained in the interior of the market (they were responsible for surveillance and assigning spaces to vendors). They disappeared towards the middle of the 20th century, just before the destruction of the central Halles location and the market's relocation to Rungis. From then on it was the president of Semmaris (the organization which administers the Rungis sight) who gave the lilies to the President of the Republic.

11. (b) Pavilion no. 8 housed the eggs and fowl market.

12. (c) The "French chicken house corporation" is at 36 quai des Orfèvres. In classic argot, it's also called the maison Poulaga. Recently, a film was released with the title *36 quai des Orfèvres* (Olivier Marchal, 2005).

13. (b) Magistrates, and also university professors, get their robes and gowns from 3 boulevard du Palais.

14. (a) Prisoners were subjected to questioning in the tower, as well as torture that gave them "good mouths" by making them talk.

15. (a) Sainte-Chapelle was constructed between 1246 and 1258, on the initiative of the pious king Saint Louis, to hold relics from the Passion. The midnight blue ceiling of the high chapel, like that of the lower chapel, is sprinkled with golden stars.

16. (b) Le Mai was a tree that the prosperous and powerful Orfèvres corporation used to plant there during the 15th century, on the first of May of each year.

17. (a) The circular rue de Viarmes surrounds the commodities exchange.

18. (a) Along the edge of the Pont-Neuf used to rise a water pump called La Samaritaine, commissioned by Henri IV to keep the Tuileries garden watered. The pump was outfitted with an astronomic clock and decorated with a bas-relief showing the good Samaritan giving a drink to Christ. The pump was destroyed in 1813 and replaced in 1900 by the department store founded by Ernest Cognacq and his wife Louise Jay.

19. (c) Toulouse was deliberately left out for reasons of symmetry. Only Bordeaux, Brest, Lille, Lyon, Marseille, Nantes, Rouen and Strasbourg have statues.

20. (c) The voyage of the obelisk from Luxor, via Gibraltar and Le Havre, lasted nearly two years and 24 days. To transport the 227-ton monolith, it was necessary to build *Le Luxor*, a boat with eight hulls and three masts, capable of crossing the Mediterranean and sailing up the Seine.

21. (b) The two pyramids share basically the same incline (51 degrees) but Khufu's is nearly ten times bigger than that of the Cour Napoléon (with sides of 34.5 m and a height of 65 m).

22. (a) The belfry of the church of Saint-Germain-l'Auxerrois has one of the most complete sets of bells in France. Installed in 1884, it includes 38 bells (covering three chromatic scales) and chimes at regular hours. The concerts given by Paris's only bell-ringer, Renaud Gagneux, attract numerous listeners to the place de l'Amiral-de-Coligny every Wednesday between 1:30 and 2:00. In addition, Luther's *Cantique* is played every day at 10:00, 12:00, 2:00, 4:00, 6:00 and 8:00 for three minutes.

23. (c) The character of Tartuffe, who brought the church and its representatives ridicule and shame, earned Molière the church's refusal of a Catholic burial. Nevertheless, a requiem mass was celebrated at Saint-Eustache for the upholsterer's son, Jean-Baptiste Poquelin, but not for the playwright.

24. (b) The station was first named, as were many others, after the road where it is situated. The rue des Pyramides owes its name to a victory of Bonaparte. He delivered the Battle of the Pyramids on the 21st of July 1798, and entered Cairo two days later.

25. (c) The status of the Louvre changed from royal residence to national museum during the revolution, under the name The Central Museum of Art.

26. (a) Counterfeiters were plunged, still living, into a vat of boiling water.

27. (c) The profession of the owners of the galerie Véro-Dodat, butchers, was the object of a number of witticisms, such as "a passage built on cervelas and sausages" and "a fine piece of art stuck between two quarters."

28. (a) Sainte-Chapelle was built by Saint Louis to house relics of the Passion, notably the crown of thorns, a 22-cm piece of the cross with a nail, an iron fragment of the Holy Lance, a bit of sponge and a tattered piece of Christ's clothing. These relics are today a part of the treasury of Notre-Dame.

29. (b) The presence of a tortoise is a nod to the slowness of justice.

30. (a) Before leaving on a crusade, Philippe Auguste had a fortified perimeter constructed to protect the city from attack by the king of England, Richard the Lionheart. The foundation of the impressive 15-meter cylindrical dungeon that can be viewed in the part of the museum called the "Louvre médiéval" is a relic of it.

2ND ARRONDISSEMENT

1. (b) The horse is reared back on its hind limbs. Its extravagantly long tail descends all the way to the ground and serves as a sort of crutch to keep the statue standing.

2. (a) Notre-Dame-de-Bonne-Nouvelle is the patron of radio and of television, which diffuse more or less happy messages through the airwaves.

3. (b) The habitants of the quarter rejoiced at the expulsion of the thugs and crooks who occupied the cour des Miracles (then situated near the current place du Caire). To bring life back to the abandoned site, it was decided that diverse privileges be given to shopkeepers who came to establish businesses there (creating a sort of duty-free zone). Thus, twice the good fortune for the inhabitants.

4. (c) 17th century Paris had 12 cours de Miracles, gathering places for crooks where even the police didn't dare to go. Numerous beggars left the squares in the morning only to return in the evening, having panhandled all day long. They then unburdened themselves of their rags and other work accessories (crutches, wooden legs, fake stumps, bloodstained sores), and returned toddlers they had rented to their nurses for the night. Blind men regained their sight and the deaf could hear anew. The miracle was accomplished!

5. (a) A carrier pigeon informed Baron Nathan de Rothschild of the defeat of Napoleon I at Waterloo, three days before the rest of the world learned. The financier was thus able to sell his stock holdings before a disastrous crash.

6. (a, b, and c) All three answers are correct. The rue des Degrés, as its name implies, is a stairway of fourteen steps. It's also the shortest road in the capital (5.75 m long).

7. (b) The prix Goncourt is awarded at Drouant on the third Monday in November, in a room on the second floor. In 1983, microphones were discovered hidden under the table. The laureate for that year was Frédérick Tristan for his novel *Les Égarés*.

8. (b) Jean sans Peur, Duke of Bourgogne, feared reprisals from his family, having himself had his brother the Duke of Orléans killed. His fears were justified: he was ultimately assassinated at Montereau, in 1419.

9. (c) The théâtre des Bouffes-Parisiens, situated on rue Monsigny. It was directed by Jean-Claude Brialy from 1986 until 2007.

10. (c) The rue Gratte-Cul was so named because of the parasites that prostitutes distributed liberally among their clients.

11. (a) The statue of General Desaix was the first public depiction of a nude person. Nude statues were, until then, reserved for the depiction of allegorical figures and gods. Desaix in his birthday suit caused such a scandal that a fence had to be built around him to accommodate the modesty of the quarter's bourgeois inhabitants until the statue could be taken away. It was melted down in 1815.

12. (a) The fake invalids snacked on soap in order to drool giant bubbles.

13. (b) The plans for the exchange were drawn by the architect Alexandre Théodore Brongniart, who died in 1813, before the completion of construction. The Greek-style building was completed by Étienne-Éloy Labarre in 1825.

14. (c) Created in 1799 on the site of the convent of the Filles-Dieu, the passage du Caire is composed of three corridors (Sainte-Foy, Saint-Denis and du Caire) totaling 370 meters in length. Originally, the gravestones of the convent's devout constituted part of the paving of the corridors.

15. (b) Vidocq, ex-convict, became the head of a private police force of former convicts who watched over the security of merchants.

16. (b) In *Voyage au bout de la nuit* and *Mort à credit*, Céline evokes the passage Choiseul, calling it the "passage des Bérésinas between the exchange and the boulevards."

17. (a) The love goddess Hathor is identifiable by her cow ears. The passage du Caire, built in 1799, is the oldest covered passage in Paris.

18. (a) The angel of the rue de Turbigo, which stretches over three stories, is the biggest of the sculptures adorning the apartment buildings of Paris. The director Agnès Varda made it the main character of her 1984 film *Les Dites Cariatides*.

19. (a) It was a brothel during the Belle Époque, operating under the name Aux Belles Poules (The Beautiful Chicks). A suggestive mosaic depicts lascivious women.

20. (b) In 1878 the avenue de l'Opéra was the first road to be equipped with electric streetlights, which replaced the gas streetlights that had been in use since the 1830s. Before that, oil lamps were hung by ropes above the Parisian boulevards.

21. (c) Lulli scraped his foot with a blow from his baton while directing his *Te Deum*. The wound became infected; Lulli refused amputation and died of gangrene.

22. (b) The Vivienne and Colbert galeries remain fiercely competitive. Although the galerie Colbert is more luxurious, Parisians prefer the galerie Vivienne.

23. (b) The proclamation of the third republic on the 4th of September 1870.

24. (b) Stern, a printer and engraver, specialized in business cards, menus, invitations and announcements as well as reproductions of coats of arms.

25. (a) The paintings represent views of Paris and of great foreign cities. The panorama inspired a whole series of "things in the round," as they were called by early 20th century observers. It was the ancestor of the georama (a globe seen from the inside), the neorama (an interior view of monuments), the diorama (a vertical painting depicting figures or landscapes lighted in a variety of ways) and even the modern Géode, in Parc de la Villette. The passage des Panoramas owes its name to an attraction of this type that was installed at its entrance.

26. (a) It was Georges Feydeau (1862-1921), whose name is borne by a road in the 2nd arrondissement.

27. (b) The croque-monsieur is a specialty originating in England. Parisians tasted it for the first time in 1850 at 23 boulevard des Capucines, in one of the first English bars in the capital.

28. (c) Stendhal suffered a stroke, from which he died the following night.

29. (b) In 1828, the former boulevard de Gand became the boulevard des Italiens, due to the fact that it abutted the theater of the Comédie italienne (today the Opéra comique).

30. (b) At 47 rue de Richelieu one could find a restaurant reserved for single women.

3RD ARRONDISSEMENT

※

1. (b) A rambuteau was a one-man public urinal in the shape of a cylinder. It owes its name to the Seine prefect who initiated numerous sanitary and beautification projects in the capital during the 19th century. Installed around 1842, these hygienic columns were also designed to welcome publicity posters on their sides, posters having been until then slapped on the walls of the capital.

2. (a) Flamel's renters had to recite one Our Father and one Hail Mary for the deceased. An inscription governing the agreement is still visible on the front of his house at 51 rue de Montmorency.

3. (a) A ménétrier was a musician, most often a violinist, who made people dance at weddings and other celebrations.

4. (c) The boulevard du Temple housed a multitude of small theaters where melodramas and the bloody spectacles Parisians were crazy about were performed. This billing is the origin of its nickname "boulevard du Crime."

5. (b) The oldest house in Paris dates from 1407. Called the maison du Haut Pignon (House of the High Gable), it belonged to Nicolas Flamel.

6. (a) Denis Papin (the pressure cooker is also known as "Papin's Pot"); **(b)** Alessando Volta (the electric battery); **(c)** The Montgolfier brothers (the hot air ballon); **(d)** Nicolas Conté (graphite pencil lead); **(e)** René de Réaumur (the alcohol thermometer); **(f)** Jacques de Vaucanson (automatons).

7. (a) This prototype with silk-sail wings, similar to those of a bat, was the object of a test flight in 1897. Clément Ader is considered the inventor of the word "avion."

8. (b) On the occasion of the bicentennial of the Conservatoire national des Arts et Métiers, François Schuiten fitted the station with riveted brass plates pierced with portholes, to give it the feeling of the Nautilus.

9. (b) The Cognaq-Jay Museum gathers works and objects dating from the 18th century in an intimate setting. Canvases by Watteau, Chardin, Fragonard and Rembrandt are shown there next to Chinese porcelains and thousands of other decorative art objects.

10. (c) Benedictines, for whom a convent existed in the area from 1633 until the end of the 18th century.

11. (c) This Pierre Combescot novel received the prix Goncourt in 1991.

12. (b) Claude Rambuteau (1781-1869) was Seine prefect under the July Monarchy; he's also responsible for the completion of the Arc de Triomphe and the Madeleine.

13. (c) The hôtel Carnavalet was inhabited by the marquise de Sévigné from 1677 to 1696. It owes its name to a corruption of Kernevenoy, the patronymic of its former owner.

14. (b) The name Salé was derisively given to this hotel whose owner, Pierre Aubert de Fontenay, held the position of "maître des gabelles." The holder of this 17th-century position was responsible for the collection of the salt tax.

15. (c) The first "mât de cocagne" was erected, coated in chicken fat provided by the numerous rotisseries of the street, which used to be known as rue "aux Oues" ("Goose Road" in old French).

4TH ARRONDISSEMENT

∞

1. (a) The sermons of Bourdaloue (1632-1704) were so long that the foresighted faithful hid earthenware vessels under their ample robes, in which they would relieve themselves, and which public malice christened "bourdaloues." To this day the term designates the 18th century–style convenience, often decorated with flowers.

2. (c) No less than six hundred people in need of cash present themselves each day at the windows of the charitable institution to obtain a secured loan. More than 90% of the loans are repaid, and the collateral recuperated, within a year.

3. (b) A small-time Île de la Cité vendor of sewing supplies, Pierre Parissot thought that there was a place for something in between the high-priced tailors and the dubious merchandise of the secondhand shops. He established a shop on the quai aux Fleurs that sold new clothes at fixed prices, and which slowly expanded until finally becoming the first real department store. The Belle Jardinière was expropriated in 1866 to permit the enlargement of the Hôtel-Dieu.

4. (b) In 1882, during the demolition of a town house on the road, a bronze vase filled with 7,882 gold pieces dating from the times of Jean le Bon and Charles V (the 14th century) appeared in the rubble. The vase and some of the coins are preserved in the musée Carnavalet.

5. (c) It was Georges Simenon, who wrote most of his detective Maigret mysteries there. Victor Hugo lived at number 6, from 1832 to 1848, in a rented apartment on the third floor of the hôtel de Roahn-Guéménée. He lived with his wife, Adèle Foucher, and their four children, before exiling himself in Jersey.

6. (b) Although equestrian statues are generally done in bronze, this one was done in white marble. It turned out to be so heavy that it needed to be supported by two crutches, one in the form of a concrete tree trunk passing through the stomach of the horse. The lifted leg is also supported.

7. (c) On the 13th of September 1800, the place des Vosges took on its current name, recognizing the exemplary civic spirit of the habitants of the Vosges département, who were the first to settle their taxes.

8. (a) The rue de Venise measures barely 2 m wide. A close runner up is the rue du Chat-qui-Pêche (at 2.5 m). The all-around prize for narrowness belongs to the sentier des Merisiers (in the 12th arrondissement), a 0.87m-wide passage (which isn't classified as a road but as a "way").

9. (b) Nicolas Flamel and his wife Pernelle were a bourgeois Parisian couple during the 15th century. Although other spouses have given their names to roads, like the physicists Pierre and Marie Curie and the painters Robert and Sonia Delaunay, those couples are listed together on the same street sign.

10. (b) The tour Saint-Jacques was rented to a shotgun shot maker. Molten lead was poured, drop-by-drop, from the top of the tower. In falling, the lead drops acquired the desired aerodynamic oval shape. They landed in great vats of cold water arranged around the base of the tower, solidifying immediately. The bell tower was also used as a watchtower during fires. Today, it is occupied by the French weather service.

11. (a) The rue du Renard-qui-Prêche makes for a charming echo of the rue du Chat-qui-Pêche (Fishing Cat Road) on the other side of the Seine.

12. (c) The Bastille was an aristocratic prison whose residents (generally men of wealth or of letters) benefited from private cells and were as well fed as they would have been on the outside. The 42 cells of the prison that symbolized royal absolutism were, however, never all occupied simultaneously.

13. (c) The name of the road was embellished over time. It is the result of a deformation of "Pute-Y-Muse" (The Prostitute Strolls There) or "Pute-Y-Musse" (The Prostitute Hides There).

14. (c) Sully, a minister and superintendent of finances, shared Henri IV's passion for architecture.

15. (c) A misinterpretation of the historical record situated Pascal's experiments on atmospheric pressure in the tour Saint-Jacques. However it was another scientist (Jacques Rohault) who conducted experiments there, while Pascal studied the weight of air from the top of one of the towers of Notre-Dame.

16. (b) The Louvre's collections start with ancient civilizations and cover a period extending to 1848; the Orsay's stretch from 1848 to 1914, and the oldest works displayed at the Pompidou Center date from 1905.

17. (b) The Pompidou Center displays its inner workings without modesty: the air conditioning circulates in the blue tubes, the green tubes correspond to the water pipes, the yellow tubes house the electrical cables and the red tubes elevators and escalators.

18. (b) The hôtel de Sens, home of the Archbishops of Sens, dates from 1475 and is one of the oldest residences in France.

19. (b) In 1871, during the Paris Commune insurrection, the Hôtel de Ville was engulfed in flames for eight days. It was later reconstructed exactly as it had been before the fire.

20. (a) During the Middle Ages the square, which gradually descends to the shore of the Seine, was the place to go to look for work. Men who were "en grève" waited there to rent their muscle to whomever wanted it. Since then, the meaning of the phrase "en grève" has been reversed — it now designates a stop in work.

21. (b) This curious clock is suspended on an iron brace wrought perpendicular to the road. It was hung in 1741.

22. (a) The horses of the Republican Guard provided the first necessary ingredient for mushroom cultivation. Today, Parisian button mushrooms come primarily from Saumur.

23. (c) 500.

24. (c) A pragmatist, Xavier Ruel sent salesman with upturned umbrellas full of trinkets to various points throughout the city in order to determine the best sales location. He tried many variations of salesmen and merchandise in order to ensure that no other factors influenced his observations. The famous shop owes its location to the results of these tests.

25. (c) It's better to lounge on the balconies of the quai de Béthune than on the quai d'Anjou or the quai de Bourbon, as the temperature there is much milder. There is an observable yearlong gap of 4-5 °C between the north and south quais of the île Saint-Louis (the latter being a veritable nest of air currents). The quai de Béthune took its current name in 1806, in honor of Maximillien de Béthune, duc de Sully, a minister to Henri IV.

26. (c) Saint-Merri's old bell is still valiantly ringing.

27. (b) The Île Saint-Louis (450 meters long) was born of the 1614 fusion of the Île aux Vaches and the Île Notre-Dame. It was for a time called Île de la France, then Île de la Fraternité sous la Révolution, before adopting its current name in 1814.

28. (b) During one of his trips to Labastide d'Armagnac (in what is currently the département of Landes), the king was lodging at the home of a friend whose windows overlooked a square featuring arcades. Charmed by the harmony of the place, he later used it as inspiration for a Parisian square.

29. (a) Jean Yanne was caught red handed unbolting a clamp used to immobilize offending vehicles. He had had a set of keys made to open the clamps and his collection, at the time of the incident, already numbered 25 pieces.

30. (a) A certain Nicolas Sauvage, a coachman by profession, bought about 20 carriages which he kept outside his home, an inn baring a sign with an effigy of Saint Fiacre. Thus, it was natural that these first rental coaches were nicknamed "fiacres" and that Saint Fiacre became the patron saint of taxis.

5TH ARRONDISSEMENT

1. (b) Around the year 500, Clovis chose Paris as a principal residence and decided he would be buried there. But it was his son Childebert I who made the city the real capital of the kingdom of the Franks, locating his treasury there. It became the definitive capital of France under the reign of Phillipe Auguste (1180-1223).

2. (a) There are in fact two women in the Panthéon, however Marie Curie is the only one honored for her work. Sophie Berthelot died on the same day as her chemist husband, and no one had the heart to separate them. Marie Curie was also the first woman named a Sorbonne professor.

3. (a) The sundial takes the form of a scallop (a coquille Saint-Jacques in French), and was produced in 1968 by Salvador Dali.

4. (a) The birth of the future Louis XIV, as wished for, occurred in

1638...after a 23-year wait. The queen didn't begrudge heaven the delay, and had the church of Val-de-Grâce built.

5. (b) Cured of a grave illness, Louis XV, true to his word, had a church built in honor of the patron of Paris, Saint Geneviève.

6. (c) A reward was offered to whomever could find a misprint in a book printed by the house. This fine piece of publicity demonstrated the degree of perfection of their technique.

7. (b) Before the 15th century, the rue de la Parcheminerie was called the rue des Écrivains.

8. (a) Bilipo is an abbreviation of Bibliothèque des literature policières (Library of Detective Novels).

9. (b) On the Left Bank, the seat of university life, teaching was conducted in Latin.

10. (c) It is Saint Geneviève, whose statue is perched atop a 14m-high pylon on the pont de la Tournelle. The stone sculpture is the work of Paul Landowski (1928).

11. (b) Geneviève incited Parisians to resist the Huns and Attila...who gave up attacking the city.

12. (b) At the théâtre de la Huchette two Eugène Ionesco pieces have played since 1957: *La Cantatrice Chauve* and *La Leçon*.

13. (b) The tapestries show the five senses and the motto "to my only desire."

14. (c) The Square Vivani's acacia (*Robinia pseudoacacia*), planted in 1601 by the botanist Robin, is the oldest of Parisian trees. Being in a bad state, it is supported by concrete braces.

15. (b) A rood screen, or jubé, is a transverse corridor elevated above the nave, used for the reading of sacred texts. The appearance of pulpits proved fatal to the rood screen, and there are only nine left in France. Their French name (jubé) comes from a Latin prayer beginning "Jube, Domine, benedicere" (Lord, grant me your blessing).

16. (b) The arènes de Lutèce were built at the beginning of the 2nd century. This amphitheatre served as both theatre and arena; it is the largest known example in Gaul from its era. More than fifteen thousand spectators could attend at one time to see animal combat, gladiator fights, dance spectacles, pantomimes, acrobatics, etc.

17. (b) So the slender spire of Sainte-Chapelle, which reaches 75 meters, can be seen on the boulevard.

18. (b) The billy clubs were nicknamed "bidules" (thingamajigs).

19. (a) To give himself an advantage in his dealings with a black-market supplier, Gabin shouted the man's identity to a sleeping Paris: "Monsieur Jambier, 45 rue Poliveau, that will be 2,000 francs now! Jambier, Jambier, Jambier!" The character is named Jamblier in the original Marcel Aymé novel.

20. (a and b) The Club Quartier-Latin pool served as a backdrop to scenes in *Bleu* (K. Kieslowski) and *Nelly et M. Arnaud* (C. Sautet).

21. (b) Charles-Michel de L'Épée (1712–1789), called the abbé de L'Épée, fought for recognition of the fact that deaf mutes were people like any other. He perfected sign language, an essential means of communication.

22. (c) The church and its cemetery were located between the rue Racine and the rue des Écoles, on the current site of the Gibert bookstore. Using the shape of the remains (most of the exhumed spinal columns were curved and presented malformations), it was deduced that it was a cemetery for hunchbacks.

23. (b) Both refused to be buried in the Panthéon. Louis Pasteur rests in Paris, at the institute that bears his name, while the general was returned to Colombey-les-Deux-Églises.

24. (b) The putrid odors emanating from the Bièvre River (back before it was put under tunnels) were called "moffettes." They were caused by the tanneries, tripe-sellers and skinners who set up shop on the banks of the river, and dumped their waste in it.

25. (c) Thus, a part of the library catalog is visible on its façade.

26. (a) Gaspard Monge (1746–1818) was a brilliant geometrician who was responsible for the creation of the École polytechnique.

27. (c) Louis Jean-Marie Daubenton (1716–1800), naturalist, introduced Merino sheep, and their high-quality wool, to France. Censier isn't a proper noun, but a corruption of the expression "sans chief" ("headless"), which used to be the name of a cul-de-sac off of the rue Mouffetard.

28. (c) The collection includes approximately 40 giant crystals, the heaviest weighing 4,000 kg, or four metric tons. This weight seems incredible in light of the fact that a crystal with a one-meter diameter is several million times rarer than a ten-cm crystal of the same type.

29. (a) It's one of the five "exceptions" among Paris's fountains, flowing in the winter as well as the summer. Water to the others is cut off from January 1st to April 1st due to risk of freezing.

30. (a) The butts, gathered in the streets or cafés by "mégotiers" (also known as "orphan gatherers") were peeled of their papers and the strands of tobacco given to tobacconists at low prices. The tobacconists would recycle them and sell them as "hand-rolled cigarettes."

6TH ARRONDISSEMENT

✕

1. (b) Germanopratins live in the Saint-Germain-des-Prés quarter.

2. (c) The name "Deux-Magots" comes from the sign of a novelty shop which used to occupy the same spot. Around 1885, the novelty shop gave way to a "café liquoriste." The two statues that decorate the seating area of the establishment still bear witness to that era.

3. (b) The outfits are made of blue cloth of varying intensities. It was the embroidery that used to be green. A sample of the original green (a color between lamp-shade green and "drap du bureau" green) is kept in the national archives. Today, embroideries range from yellow to blue, by way of a whole range of greens.

4. (c) Jean-Bart, like Surcouf (who has a road in the 7th arrondissement), was a corsair: a ship's captain authorized by the king to pursue and board enemy merchant vessels. The corsair is not to be confused with the pirate, an adventurer pillaging for his own benefit. "Flibustier" was a name for the pirates who ravaged the Caribbean Sea and the area around the coasts of South America.

5. (b) The Institut de France, whose goal is to connect diverse fields of instruction, was founded by Richelieu in 1635. It houses the Académie française, the Académie des inscriptions et belles-lettres, the Académie des sciences, the Académie des beaux arts and the Académie des sciences morales et politiques.

6. (a) Jean Rostand (who worked on amphibians) had a sword decorated with toads. Certain academy members refuse all military insignia as incompatible with their pacifist beliefs, choosing not to wear the sword. Although women who belong to an Académie are exempt, Hélène Carrère d'Encausse, a fencer, chose to wear a sword like her peers.

7. (b) One refers to the "obverse" of a medal. The making of coins has since moved to the south of France, and the hôtel de la Monnaie now strikes only medals.

8. (b) The Procope served all sorts of sensational drinks, including coffee, tea, hot chocolate, fruit juice, lemonade and exotic wines. A mecca of intellectual life, it welcomed encyclopedists, revolutionaries (it was here that they first wore the highly patriotic Phrygian bonnet) and then, during the next century, romantics.

9. (a) The meter, which facilitated mastery of the metric system and uniformity of measure, was adopted in 1795 by the National Convention.

10. (b) In the 10th century, the space which stretches from the current Luxembourg Garden to the Denfert-Rochereau crossroads was occupied by a valley planted with vineyards and orchards, so verdant that it was christened "Val Vert" (Green Valley). Val Vert, over the course of time, became Vauvert. A château was built there, which ultimately fell into ruin. The ruins were long thought to be haunted. The expression "au diable vauvert" describes a lost and unadvisable place.

11. (b) Although the Closerie des Lilas is certainly a serious contender for the title of "*café littéraire*," it is located at Port-Royal.

12. (a) Ossip Zadkine was a French sculptor of Russian origin.

13. (a) The lycée Fénelon was the first to open its doors to young women.

14. (a) Georges Perec, in February 1974.

15. (a) The intersection of rue Bernard-Palissy and rue du Sabot is an old-style crossroads. Both the right and left turns have always been difficult to negotiate. In the early 1900s, the examiners for the license to drive a team of horses used it to judge the competence of candidates.

16. (a) The composition, called *Allégorie de la Céramique*, adorned the pavilion of the Sèvres factory during the 1900 World's Fair before being put up at the site.

17. (c) Odéon means "room where one sings." Today the word designates a building with multiple tiers used for listening to music and, in Paris, a theatre constructed in the 18th century.

18. (c) Pierre Curie succumbed to a traffic accident.

19. (b) Mabillon was a Benedictine monk who wrote divers treatises on diplomacy in the 12th century; he's considered the founder of the discipline.

20. (b) Situated at the crossroads of the rue de Rennes and the rue de Bonaparte, opposite the place Saint-Germain-des-Prés, this bronze fountain depicts the cracking of the ice on the Saint Lawrence River in spring. It was offered to France by the government of Quebec in 1984.

7TH ARRONDISSEMENT

⚜

1. (c) The passageways of the Parisian sewer stretch exactly 2,389 km. A museum is devoted to them (opposite 93 quai d'Orsay).

2. (a) Around the year 1816 Réné Laennec invented the stethoscope, which revolutionized methods of auscultation.

3. (c) Contrary to a tenacious legend, the pillars of the Eiffel Tower don't sit on caissons filled with water. At the time of construction, hydraulic jacks were used to regulate the level of the four pillars and to maintain their connection to the 1st floor. They were later replaced with caissons filled with concrete.

4. (c) Saint Vincent de Paul rests, mummified, in a glass shrine in the chapel which bears his name. The "natural" mummy of Henri IV is housed in the basilica of Saint-Denis. The body is perfectly preserved, but can't be seen under the slab of his tomb.

5. (a and c) It was discovered that the paint on the base of the tower was deteriorating less quickly than that on the rest of the structure. Since that realization, the area from the ground to the first floor has been repainted every ten years, and the area from the first floor to the top every five years.

6. (b) Just one year of entry ticket sales was enough to pay off the investments necessary for the construction of the Eiffel Tower.

7. (b) This statue of Napoleon was situated, at the time, on the current site of La Défense. It was submerged in the Seine as a last resort, near the pont de Neuilly. Its forced bath lasted four months... but did save it!

8. (a) The recreated sites were fortified maritime cities, border areas and other strategic places such as Mont-Saint-Michel. The 1/600 scale reproductions were rigorously exact: not a window or a chimney was missing. They served to simulate sieges and attacks and to prepare urban construction. The collection, formerly classified as a military secret, has occupied the attic of the Invalides since 1777. There are also relief maps at Lille's palais des Beaux-Arts.

9. (b) It took 12.65 kg of gold, in the form of very fine sheets, to completely re-gild the lead decor of the dome.

10. (a) The name of André Citroën was spelled out in luminous letters 20 m tall, in six colors, arranged on the four sides of the tower. The effect was visible for 38 km.

11. (b) The Eiffel tower belongs to the city of Paris.

12. (a) The frescoes that adorn the walls of the Far Eastern Room show episodes from the Sino-Japanese War, in which the Chinese soldiers seem to be suffering a bitter defeat.

13. (b) Valentin-Haüy founded a school for blind children. The museum that bears his name (at 5 rue Duroc) displays different lettering systems, globes, and geographic maps in relief, as well as braille alphabets.

14. (b) They engage in private prayer before the relics of their martyred brothers in the salle des Martyrs d'Extrême-Orient (The Martyrs of the Far East Room) in the chapelle de la Mission (128 rue du Bac).

15. (b) The tower was used to support antennas starting in 1904. During the first World War, it was of great use to the French army, who made it a military radio communications center.

16. (a) The tower might just as easily be called a sunflower as, to flee the sun, it curves its summit 18 cm away from the sun, only to return to its starting point in the evening. In cases of great cold it plays the snail, retracting its antenna 15 cm. In high winds, its summit oscillates only 12 cm.

17. (a) The Most Noble Order of the Garter, founded in 1348 by King Edward III, is the most important English chivalric order. The museum of the Légion d'honneur collects royal, imperial, military and religious orders, as well as both civil and military awards and decorations, from France and abroad.

18. (c) A rhinoceros, a horse and an elephant, all in bronze, guard the square outside the musée d'Orsay.

19. (a) A pensive Dante considering his *Inferno* is also to be found at the top of Rodin's *La Porte de l'Enfer*.

20. (b) The president's desk in the chamber of the National Assembly is called his "perch." Situated on high, it dominates the debating chamber.

8TH ARRONDISSEMENT

⚜

1. (a) Horse races took place on the Champs-Élysées until the creation of the Longchamp racecourse in 1860.

2. (b) It was a pleasure to ride along the Champs-Élysées. Thus coachmen, carriage merchants, and saddlers naturally set themselves up there. At the end of the 19th century, the humorist Craft remarked that: "The Champs-Élysées was the horse's greatest conquest!" Coachbuilders were the logical successors of horse merchants and arrived around the year 1900. In the 1930s, all the great automobile manufacturers showed their latest models on the avenue. The headquarters of AAA and the Automobile Club of France are also located there.

3. (b) Fortunately, The Horses of Marly stayed in France.

4. (b) From 1880 to 1914, the July 14th parade took place at Longchamp, before adopting the Champs-Élysées in 1915.

5. (b) The "questioning" was torture inflicted on the accused before judgment. Miromesnil worked to humanize the justice system.

6. (a) The flame is rekindled every evening at 6:30 by one of the nine hundred French veterans associations. The ceremony has never ceased, even during the occupation from 1940 to 1944. The coffin of the unknown soldier was chosen randomly from among eight others. Between the First and Second World Wars, prankster students from the École polytechnique took a collection to benefit the family of the unknown soldier, reaping no small sum.

7. (a) The flame must be rekindled as soon as possible but, according to the rules, it must be done in a ceremonial rite, performed standing at attention to the sound of bugle and drum.

8. (a) These globetrotters covered the world in twenty years. Their home (which has become the musée Jacquemart-André) is located at 158 boulevard Haussmann.

9. (c) They are required to be white. Advertisers and merchants must conform to the decision of uniformity taken in the interest of esthetics. Even the McDonald's had to swap its yellow M for a white one, making it the only exception in the world. Only pharmacies are allowed to break the rule.

10. (a, b or c) Whichever you like! The debate goes back to the 1930s, no solution having ever achieved unanimity.

11. (c) She had planted alfalfa in her park. With famine looming, all land had to be sowed with "productive" and nourishing plants, like wheat. It was an era of sharp cutbacks...

12. (b) "Pieds-humides." In 1887, a rich stamp collector left the site of the Carré Marigny to the city of Paris, on the condition that it authorize the establishment of an open-air market. The market, located on the avenue Gabriel, takes place on Thursdays, Saturdays, Sundays and holidays from 10 a.m. to 6 p.m. A large number of merchants are to be found there, offering a wide selection of stamps from around the world, post cards and phone cards.

13. (b) Montaigne. The rich clients of the eponymous avenue's luxury boutiques might learn something from the maxim!

14. (b) In 1886 the avenue was covered with pavers made of wood, considered a luxury material worthy of the avenue. Made slick by the rain, the oil from cars, and wear, the surface ultimately proved impractical and was the cause of numerous accidents. It was replaced in 1938 with the granite we know today.

15. (b) In his play *Topaze* (1928), Marcel Pagnol makes reference to the curious movements of the wheeled, horse-drawn urinals, freshly installed on the Champs-Élysées.

16. (b) While all churches (as well as synagogues and mosques) have their nave oriented to the east (and Jerusalem), the Madeleine is the exception. It is oriented north-south in order to offer a view of the rue Royale.

17. (a) There was a fear that the heat wave might provoke disorder among the spectators and soldiers.

18. (a) In 1810, Napoleon I organized a parade for his marriage with Marie-Louise; it was the first historic procession to use the avenue. The second, less joyous occasion was the return of the emperor's ashes in 1840.

19. (a) The Lido is a Venetian beach. The Lido des Champs-Élysées, created in 1928, was a spa nicknamed "the Paris beach." It was a veritable city of artificial underground bodies of water with a decor consisting of canals and gondolas, surrounding a hammam and an immense pool the color of seawater.

20. (a) The members of the Champs-Élysées committee feared that the low prices of the boutique Rosemonde would attract too common a clientele. The debate resurfaced in 1982 with the establishment of the first fast food restaurants on the avenue.

9TH ARRONDISSEMENT

✖

1. (a) The 150 commissioners, also called Savoyards, wear a black jacket with gold buttons and a carmine collar embroidered with their number. They are recruited by committee, and the conditions for application are strict: they must have at least one Savoyard or Haut-Savoyard parent, be less than 30 years old, be forceful and tactful, have a clean criminal record, have a truck driver's license, and complete a probationary period of six months.

2. (a) The Cave of Thieves was the first wax museum in the world (circa 1780). It was followed by Mme Tussaud's London museum (circa 1795), and then by the musée Grévin (1882), which was inspired by Tussaud's.

3. (b) The effigy was regularly stabbed with pins during the 1960s.

4. (b) The first traffic light, only one color, was red. It was accompanied by a horn, activated by an agent. It took ten years for the green and orange lights to appear.

5. (b) Napoleon III was the target of an attack as he approached the rue Le Peletier opera on January 14, 1858. Italian anarchists threw several incendiary devices into his procession. Miraculously spared, the emperor demanded an opera with a secure entrance and a clear surrounding area. The Garnier was outfitted with a private entrance (on the left side), including a coach ramp leading directly to the imperial box.

6. (c) The crystal and bronze chandelier weighs six tons. It has approximately 400 bulbs.

7. (a) The chandelier's counterweight broke; six tons of bronze and crystal fell on the spectators, causing one death and multiple injuries.

8. (c) The buildings' architects were inspired by the style of Greek antiquity. The quarter, situated between the rues de Clichy, de Châteaudun, Chaptal and des Martyrs, was the private retreat of writers and artists (notably Sand, Chopin, Ingres, Delacroix, Liszt and Lamartine) from the end of the empire until about 1860. They met every Friday in Ary Scheffer's pavilion, which is today a museum: the musée de la vie Romantique, on rue Chaptal.

9. (b) The church was very close to the national conservatory of music, and it was thought that the clocks would disturb the musicians at work. Poor Saint Cecilia, the patron saint of musicians, was condemned to silence!

10. (a) It was to provide the families of the four hundred workers of the nearby rue Condorcet gas factory with housing that was clean and spacious (with central walkways, sky lights, and gardens), and that had communal equipment (such as a wash house, a nursery and baths). The workers, however, shunned the complex, considering it much like a prison, as it was watched over by a caretaker. The buildings, on 58 rue du Rochechouart, are still lived in.

11. (a) The spectators saw the departure of the workers from the Lumière factories. The date of the projection is considered the official date of the birth of cinema.

12. (a) A chapel dedicated to Saint Rita, the patron saint of prostitutes and lost causes.

13. (a) Anvers. *Le Dernier Métro* came out in 1980.

14. (b) In the 17th century, the square was crossed by wagons loaded with plaster from the Montmartre quarries.

15. (a) Francis Blanche.

16. (a) The bust of the caricaturist seems to show him going over his subject from head to toe in the moment before putting pen to paper. A few of his familiar models (Pierrot, a milliner, Harlequin, lorette) are shown in bas-relief, forming a circle around the pedestal.

17. (c) The group of marble women is called: *Saint Catherine, Parisian Worker*.

18. (c) One-way traffic first appeared in 1909 in the 9th arrondissement. It is still in use on the parallel roads of the area.

19. (c) On that day, the pilot Jule Védrines succeeded in the exploit of putting his monoplane down on the roof of the Galeries Lafayette. The same site was again chosen as a landing spot on the 4th of July 1948, this time for a helicopter.

20. (b) These artists, frequenters of the Nouvelle Athènes quarter, refused to receive the Légion d'honneur.

10TH ARRONDISSEMENT

1. (c) Eighty-four people died of asphyxiation in the Couronnes station fire. But for the stinginess of passengers who lingered on site to claim a refund of their three sous (about 15 euro cents) the number of victims wouldn't have been so high. After the catastrophe the metro was for a while nicknamed the "nécropolitan."

2. (c) The countess Élisa Laribosière, who had no heir, left the majority of her fortune for the establishment of the Parisian hospital that received her name.

3. (b) Hairdressers and wig makers come to restock on the passage de l'Industrie.

4. (b) Éventaillistes, who collaborate with other artisans (seamstresses, gilders, lace makers) to care for the "residents" of the musée de l'Éventail (at 2 boulevard de Strasbourg).

5. (b) The canal Saint-Martin is broken by nine locks that function like a staircase, making light work of the gradient. It climbs 25 m over 4 km between the Seine and the La Villette pond, amounting to 3 m per lock.

6. (c) The installation of more modern systems has reduced the time spent in the lock to 20 minutes, instead of the 30 it took not long ago.

7. (b) The morbid Montfaucon gallows stood not far from it, from the 13th century until 1761. The terror of crooks and scoundrels, the gallows consisted of two levels and could "welcome" 60 nooses at the same time!

8. (a) The passerelle Bichat is nearest to the Hôtel du Nord, situated at 102 quai de Jemmapes. The scene from the Marcel Carné film, however, was shot in a studio.

9. (b) A certain Monsieur Pannoussamy, from Puducherry, opened the passage's first grocery store in 1972. He was joined, six years later, by 15 or so Pakistani restaurateurs.

10. (a) The two victory arches were constructed under the orders of Louis XIV, in honor of his victories at the Rhine and at Franche-Comté in 1672 and 1674. They stand on the site of two entrances to Paris from the former border wall of Charles V.

11. (c) It was too close to the neighboring stations. The station was temporarily used to house the homeless. The platform still has advertisements on its earthenware tiles, installed as demonstration models for advertisers.

12. (b) In a move linked to the Dreyfus affair, the militant anti-Semite Jules Guérin and 15 or so collaborators barricaded themselves inside the building, resisting law enforcement, who encircled them for 38 days. The besieged men were replenished with fresh supplies by sympathizers on neighboring roofs. The strange event has been remembered by posterity under the name "Fort Chabrol."

13. (a) Sandwiched between two apartment blocks, it measures 1.2 m wide and 5 m tall, blocking an old alley between the rue du Château-d'Eau and the rue du Faubourg-Saint-Martin.

14. (a) On Sunday, the 10th of November 1940, Jacques and his friends were returning from a wedding. They were walking through the black of night, civil defense requirements having outlawed the use of all exterior lights, when they were stopped by a group of German soldiers. Everyone scattered, but Jacques, who was spotted because of his great height, was arrested. The soldiers demanded that he give the names of his comrades, which he refused to do to his last breath. He was the first French civilian shot by the Germans, on December 23, 1940. A street near his home at 3 boulevard de Magenta was baptized with his name.

15. (c) The form, color, limpidity and composition of the castings of skin diseases in the wax museum of medical horrors is strikingly real.

16. (b) Jacques Hittorff, the favorite architect of Napoleon III, was hated by Haussmann, who restricted him to building the station at a remove from the great roads constructed to serve the new railroad stations. The baron and prefect wanted to punish the architect for having opposed him on the financing of work on the bois de Boulogne.

17. (a) The front of the lodge is decorated with Art Nouveau–style ceramics from the earthenware works at Choisy-le-Roi, the same suppliers who provided more than 100,000 square meters of ceramic tile to the nascent metro.

18. (a) The first gasworks in France was installed in the gardens of the chapel. 1,500 rifles provided by the minister of war were used as pipes. The new "hydrogen gas" lighting transformed December 25th 1819's midnight mass in the hospital's chapel into a veritable extravaganza.

19. (a) The famous Montfaucon gallows, principal gallows of the kings of France, was situated on a hillock near the route de Meaux (currently the rue de la Grange-aux-Belles) and the modern place du Colonel-Fabien. Erected at the request of Enguerrand de Marigny (who was himself hanged there), it was transferred to La Villette in 1761 and destroyed in 1790.

20. (b) The rue de l'Aqueduc spans the tracks of the gare de l'Est.

11TH ARRONDISSEMENT

1. (c) The spectacular sundial is one of the largest in Europe. The work of Daniel Bry (1986), it is surrounded by terraces. The shadow of its 6m-high needle projects onto ten abstract statues corresponding to ten hours (from 8:00 a.m. to 5:00 p.m.).

2. (a) Each of the caryatids has the body of a child.

3. (b) The partners François Richard and Joseph Lenoir ran the first cotton factory in Paris at the beginning of the 18th century. The station is often thought to refer to a single person as, after Lenoir's death, François Richard added his friend's name to his own.

4. (b) Christophe Philippe Oberkampf founded the first French factory to produce printed cloths (called toiles de Jouy) in the middle of the 18th century.

5. (b) In the northern hemisphere, the water drains counterclockwise.

6. (a) The association, founded in 1991, gave itself the mission of promoting vine cultivation on terraces and balconies, and uniting all Parisians who cultivate at least one vine (even in a pot). Its headquarters is at 42 rue Léon-Frot.

7. (b) Jules Verne's futuristic novel *Paris in the 20th Century*, made available to the public by the great-grandson of the author, wasn't published until 1994. The rue Jules-Verne crosses through the 11th arrondissement.

8. (a) The reputation of Nicolas de Blégny, apothecary and surgeon to Queen Marie-Thérèse and to the Duke of Orléans, rested largely on health potions stolen from his colleagues. His frauds caused him to lose his title of King's physician and, in 1693, to be imprisoned. He nevertheless remains famous for having popularized the use of cinchona and for having demonstrated the therapeutic virtues of three drinks: tea, coffee and hot chocolate.

9. (a) Every Saturday from 10:00 a.m. to 6:00 p.m., artisans would come to sell the fruits of their labor in the open air (the practice was stopped in 1906).

10. (a) The church, built during the 17th century, was expanded from 1760 to 1764 with a chapel (featuring columns, statues, bas-reliefs and a frieze) decorated by Paolo Antonio Brunetti, a theater decorator, in an elaborate trompe-l'oeil. The monumental backdrop is the largest of its era and genre to have survived.

11. (a) No one knows how long the giant red bottle has been perched on the roof of the café at the corner of the boulevard and the rue Moufle. When Robert Doisneau photographed it in 1961, the mark of the aperitif Picon could still be seen on the sticker. The bottle is now completely naked.

12. (c) The famous investigator and commissioner Jules Maigret lived in an apartment at 132 boulevard Richard-Lenoir.

13. (b) The five granite pavers submerged in the ground recall the somber time when the "the widow" presided outside the la Roquette prison.

14. (b) In 1783, François Pilâtre de Rozier built a hot air balloon there out of cloth and glued paper that, on the 15th of October, lifted itself 80 m from the ground.

15. (c) Citizen Hébert proposed to demolish all the steeples in the capital; according to him, they insulted the uniformity of roofs with their disparate heights.

16. (a) The famous colonnes Morris were created to prevent theatre posters from being put up on Haussmann's beautiful apartment buildings. Today, they glow at night and some revolve.

17. (a) The Prosper of the song, king of the street, was a notorious pimp, and the ladies in question the instruments of his guilty trade.

18. (b) The inventor of Monopoly was American. Today, there exist multiple French versions of the game, putting Lyon, the Côte d'Azur, Guadeloupe, Martinique, Réunion and countless other locales up for sale.

19. (c) The recyclers of intestines were called boyautiers or boyaudiers.

20. (a and b) Lines 8 and 9 are tied with 37 stations each.

12TH ARRONDISSEMENT

※

1. (c) The 1982 Michel Le Corre fountain shows a blue whale. Its polyester resin frame is covered in mosaic.

2. (b) It was Taine who said: "The way to bore oneself is to know where you're going and how you're getting there." You can verify the maxim yourself by walking randomly around the city: your wanderings will take you to unexpected corners of the capital in spite of yourself. The first quote is from Cioran, the last from Henri Rochefort.

3. (a) The Quinze-Vingts hospital was founded in 1254 by Saint Louis to welcome 300 unfortunate crusaders who were blinded during the holy war.

4. (c) Paris-Ventimiglia. The restaurant is classified in the inventory of historical monuments for its decor.

5. (b) 863 km long, the Paris-Marseille line (also called the Imperial Line), has linked the three leading urban areas in France since 1857.

6. (b) It was a scene from *Nikita* that was shot there, in 1990; in it Anne Parillaud prepares to execute a "contract" (a paid murder) in the restaurant.

7. (b) Approximately ten Neolithic canoes were found, carved from the trunk of a single oak, each 6 m to 7 m long. Carbon dating puts them around the years 4482–4445 BC. A branch of an ancient river once passed through the quarter, whose soil had never been excavated. The canoes made for an excellent find as such objects normally are very poorly preserved. They were accompanied by hunters' bows, stone tools, pottery and animal bones over 6,000 years old.

8. (b) In the "canyonaustrate," water cascades into a naturally formed canyon with an area of over 1700 square meters.

9. (b) It all started in 957, when monks flaunted their wealth by distributing small pieces of gingerbread during the week of Easter. Fairground workers and acrobats joined them in 1719 and the "gingerbread fair" was established on the place du Trône (currently place de la Nation). It moved in 1964, setting up on the Reuilly lawn in the bois de Vincennes.

10. (a and b) The International Buddhist Institute includes a Tibetan temple (founded in 1985) and two African huts (formerly the pavilions of Togo and Cameroon at the colonial exhibition in 1931), one of which houses a 9m-tall Buddha covered in gold leaf — the largest in Europe.

11. (c) Antoine Chaligny (who died in 1666) belonged to a family of founders from Lorraine; General Faidherbe was governor of Senegal. It's also worth noting that the name Ledru-Rollin belonged to one person (Alexandre Auguste Ledru-Rollin), a lawyer and French politician (1807-1874).

12. (a) If Auteuil is the home of the obstacle and Longchamp the home of the gallop, Vincennes's specialty is the trot, either mounted (the jockey on the horse) or harnessed (the horse pulls a sulky, led by a driver).

13. (c) Most of Guimard's kiosks evoke dragonfly wings, but two stations — Étoile and Bastille — enjoy particularly extravagant entrances. These veritable little pavilions include façades with panels of enameled lava, framed in cast iron jambs. The Bastille kiosk, with its multiple roofs set back from one another, took the form of a pagoda. It was destroyed in 1962.

14. (b) The first test of automatic entrance gates.

15. (b) In this Jules Dalou sculpture, a woman with a dynamic gait, who symbolizes the republic, seems to balance on a ball or perhaps a globe as she walks.

16. (b) The sentier des Merisiers, a pathway between the rue du Niger and the boulevard Soult (in the 12th arrondissement) measures 87 cm wide. The passage is followed by the rue de Venise (in the 4th arrondissement) the width of which barely reaches 2 m.

17. (a) It reads: "1726. Last milepost. From the reign of Louis XV. By order of the king. Explicit prohibition is made of building from this milepost and its limits to the nearest town, under penalties brought by the declarations of his majesty in the years 1724 and 1726." The king wanted to limit the anarchic expansion of Paris.

18. (c) The Richelieu wing, along the rue de Rivoli. The Minister of Finances moved to Bercy in 1989, into a building equipped with diverse security systems that make it a modern day fortress. Everything is provided for in case of extreme situations: grass moats protect the stone fountains, there are grills that are resistant to strong forces, a heliport permits the evacuation of the premises by air, and finally a dock protected by pillars offers retreat by river. The enclosure where taxes on merchandise entering Paris were kept in the 19th century stood here until 1984. Ironically, the same site is where revenue taxes — the modern equivalent of the merchandise tax? — are now collected!

19. (b) In the 16th century, a curious epidemic hit the inhabitants of the area, whose arms were covered with red blotches and marks similar to flea bites. The illness was cured by a miraculous soothing balm, cooked up by a cleric. The village of Picque-Puce (Fly Bite) stretched north from the modern porte de Picpus up to Charonne.

20. (c) The "Toureaux affair," which generated a great deal of press in its time, is still shrouded in shadow today.

13TH ARRONDISSEMENT

⨯

1. (a) One can see the words "They're crazy, these Romans!" (from the popular *Astérix* comics) in black in a white speech bubble.

2. (b and c) Only a portion of the books are freely available in the reading rooms; half of the rest of the collection is left in the towers (from the eighth to the eighteenth floor, the floors whose blinds are closed) and the other half in the base (on four levels between the esplanade and the garden level). The most popular works are put in the base, the least requested in the towers.

3. (c) The books come to readers by way of three hundred carriers which travel on an 8-km circuit of tracks fixed to the ceiling.

4. (a) The Bièvre was covered in 1912.

5. (c) The waters of the Bièvre had the peculiarity of setting colors remarkably well, which made them attractive to dyers. The Gobelin family, which had been set up on the river since 1443, was famous for the inimitable scarlet red it produced.

6. (a) It was the scientist Blaise Pascal who created the carriage company, which charged 5 sols a ride.

7. (b) The Marguerite Durand Library (at 79 rue Nationale) has a mission focusing on women and feminism.

8. (a) The école Estienne, situated on the boulevard Auguste-Blanqui, owes its name to Robert Estienne, printer to François I, who elevated typography to the level of art.

9. (c) Until the 1860s annexation of the suburbs, Paris had only 12 arrondissements; thus, it was impossible to marry at the town hall of the 13th arrondissement, and the expression ironically referred to couples living in uncommitted union. Upon the new division into 20 arrondissements, the current 16th arrondissement flatly refused the number 13 (which should logically have been assigned to it) not out of superstition, but because of the shady reputation.

10. (c) The baron Jean-Nicolas Corvisart de Marets (1755–1821) was Napoleon's personal doctor.

11. (c) A "chevaleret" is a tool that was used by the numerous tanners who occupied the quarter in the 18th century.

12. (a) Tolbiac is a city in the Rhineland, where the Franks emerged victorious from a battle with the Alamans in 496.

13. (a) The gare d'Orléans.

14. (b) Austerlitz, where the battle delivered by Napoleon I over the Austrians and Russians unfolded, was a Moravian village, in the modern Czech Republic.

15. (b) The pont Masséna (which carries the ring road over the upper reaches of the Seine) measures 492.48 m from one abutment to the other.

16. (c) The rector Sébastien Charléty put everything in place for the Paris University Club's acquisition of the stadium, unveiled in 1939, that today bears his name. It was entirely — and magnificently — rebuilt in 1994 by the architects Henri and Bruno Gaudin.

17. (a) In this Léo Malet novel, Nestor Burma investigates the death of a vagabond.

18. (b) *Le Trou* (1960) was Jacques Becker's last film.

19. (a) The entrance to this subterranean road is located at 70 avenue d'Ivry. A Buddhist temple is located at number 37.

20. (b) The "new national library" is the result of a project by Dominique Perrault, chosen in 1989 following an international competition. The opening took place from 1996 to 1998.

14TH ARRONDISSEMENT

⋙

1. (a) Bordered by blank walls, the rue Émile-Richard cuts the Montparnasse cemetery in half. The only number, 1, corresponds to the address of a funerary florist and stone-cutter.

2. (b) Apollo and the nine muses, to whom the Corinthian massif was a place of residence. In the 17th century there was, on the site of the modern Montparnasse quarter, a mound of rubble surrounded by open air cafés, where partying students came to sober up. Their inebriation inspired such clever rhymes that the place was derisively nicknamed "Montparnasse."

3. (a) The only victim was a flower-seller whose stall was set up on the sidewalk, in front of the station. The dramatic event is immortalized by photographs in which the locomotive can be seen suspended halfway through the glass wall of the station.

4. (a) The moving walkway measures 185 m long.

5. (b) The Montparnasse Tower has 59 floors (not counting the terrace on the roof), for a total height of 210 m.

6. (a) The climber made the 210 m ascent in 1 hour 20 minutes through a 100 km/h wind. As soon as he was released he dashed over to Toronto to tackle the Canadian National Tower, measuring 553 m.

7. (b) Monsieur Pigeon is the inventor of the lamp which bares his name (a gasoline lamp). The monument shows the husband and wife lying side by side in their marriage bed: Madame is sleeping under a lace bonnet while Monsieur, leaning at her side, holds his accounts book.

8. (a) Its metallic architecture was meant to remind workers of a factory...so that they felt truly at home in the house of the Lord.

9. (a) In an imposing cenotaph in the 27th division, Baudelaire is depicted as a threatening vampire-like creature, fists clenched under his chin. It is, however, on the other side of the cemetery, in the 6th division, that the poet actually rests, under a pillar topped with a simple cross.

10. (c) The skeleton of the unfortunate Philibert Aspairt, a doorman by trade, was found eleven years later by workers from a team of surveyors, and identified by the ring of keys he carried.

11. (a) A black line painted on the ceiling of the tunnels.

12. (a) The December 2005 census counted 2,144,700 Parisians. The remains in the catacombs correspond to about six million people, or about three times more skeletons than living Parisians.

13. (c) A thick pillar covered in skulls and tibias is called the "barrel."

14. (b) Chemical tests being at the time nonexistent, trout, renowned for their sensitivity to the purity of water, served as a good indicator of the quality of the water in the reservoirs.

15. (a) The lake had barely finished being filled before it drained entirely, on the very day of its opening, probably due to the earth settling. Suspected of malfeasance and dishonored, the job's overseer committed suicide shortly after.

16. (b) The place name evokes bygone times when, the windmills of the Bièvre having failed, the premises had no inhabitants outside of the rodents, who were left with barely a grain to chew.

17. (c) Ricardo Bofill baptized his fountain *The Crucible of Time*.

18. (b) The Paris Observatory, devoted to the observation of diverse celestial and atmospheric phenomena, also carries out the announcement of the time by a talking clock, as it houses the International Time Bureau.

19. (b) Neither iron nor wood were used in the construction of the Observatory, to avoid interfering with the magnetic needles and to limit the risk of fire.

20. (b) The RER B line partially picks up the trail of the old Sceaux line.

15TH ARRONDISSEMENT

1. (a) The Saint-Lambert quarter, to the south, corresponds to the old village of Vaugirard. Sainte-Marguerite is a quarter in the 11th arrondissement and Saint-Victor a quarter in the 5th.

2. (a, b and c) All three answers are correct. The liturgy unfolds according to the Tridentine rite (that of the council of Trent), also called the rite of Saint Pius V. This means that the mass is said in Latin and that the sequence of events follows that of before the revolution. One or two times a year (on the first Sunday in May or in November) the parishioners can come have their pets blessed. This "service" has been in existence since 1994.

3. (c) To better link his name to that of his wife, Cléopâtre Sevastos. The Bourdelle museum was built in the workshops the artist occupied from 1884 until 1929. Bourdelle was the assistant of Auguste (not Antoine) Rodin from 1893 to 1903.

4. (a) There were two trees on the land destined to welcome the orthodox Saint-Séraphin-de-Sarov church. As the church is dedicated to a saint who lived as a hermit in the forest, no one had the heart to cut them down. Although one is dead (its trunk remains), the other is thriving.

5. (a) The morillon is a black grape, called the pinot tête-de-nègre, which used to be cultivated at the site. A vine of the morillon variety still flourishes today on a patch of land in the Georges-Brassens park.

6. (b) Eighty varieties of fragrant, medicinal and aromatic plants mix their perfumes in this garden of smells. One can walk through it with one's eyes closed, navigating by odor and by the sound of water drops that punctuate the route.

7. (c) The old wine rotunda from the 1900 World's Fair is a polygonal building in the shape of a hive. Salvaged in 1902 by the sculptor Alfred Boucher, it became a refuge for numerous artists (particularly those from eastern Europe) who Boucher called his bees. The hive housed, among others, Léger, Chagall, Soutine, Modigliani, Zadkine, Apollinaire and Cendrars. Today listed on the inventory of historic monuments, it still welcomes artists.

8. (b) Aristide Boucicaut, founder of Bon Marché, had revolutionary and futuristic ideas. In 1863, he instituted open entry to his department store without obligation to purchase; fixed, posted prices; specialized departments; and the practices of reimbursement and returns. He had also, previous to opening Le Bon Marché, implemented social measures for his employees, such as Sundays off and benefits.

9. (a, b and c) The three answers are correct. The colors are associated with a metal, a planet, a day of the week, and also a form of water and a sense. They are:
Blue Garden: copper, Venus, Friday, rain and smell.
Green Garden: tin, Jupiter, Thursday, springs and hearing.
Orange Garden: mercury, Mercury, Wednesday, streams and touch.
Red Garden: iron, Mars, Tuesday, waterfalls and taste.
Silver Garden: silver, the moon, Monday, rivers and sight.
Golden Garden: gold, the sun, Sunday, evaporation and...the sixth sense.

10. (b) The Javel village and quay far predate the cleaning agent which shares their name in French. There used to be a Javel island, which was reattached to dry land around the 17th century. It owed its name to an accumulation of vegetal detritus on its land, similar to bundles of wheat ("javelles," in French). The bleach factory was built in 1777.

11. (a) The Charles-Michels station opens onto the place Beaugrenelle. The place bears a name invented in the 19th century, to attract clients, by real estate agents of the Grenelle quarter at the time of its urbanization.

12. (b) It's a recreation of the Croizic lighthouse, built on the initiative of the owners of the fishmonger's across the street.

13. (a) Jean-Joseph-Alexandre Falguière (1831–1900) was one of the most famous sculptors of his time. He taught at the École des Beaux-Arts and was honored with numerous public commissions.

14. (b) The square was for a long time nothing but a wasteland, the territory of stray cats, but also the place where Miró had his workshops. Two steps away, on rue Blomet, was the mythical Bal nègre, where Josephine Baker performed.

15. (c) The old Grenelle station became Bir-Hakeim in 1949, in memory of the battle that was fought in June 1942, at an oasis in the Libyan desert, between the soldiers of General Koenig and Italian and German troops. The Passy viaduct also changed its name in 1949, becoming the pont de Bir-Hakeim.

16. (a) The words and music to the song are by Charles Aznavour (1973). Pablo de Sarasate (1844–1908), who has a road named after him in the 15th arrondissement, was a Spanish violinist and composer.

17. (b) It is a 1/5 scale reduction.

18. (c) The statue, unveiled on the 4th of July 1889, was supposed to have been turned to the west, facing the United States. It would, however, have been necessary to proceed with the ceremony from a boat, which President Carnot refused categorically, in the name of the dignity of the Republic. It wasn't until 1937 that it was turned on its pedestal.

19. (a and c) The "year and a day" rule is no longer in use for reasons both empirical (few objects are claimed past a few weeks) and technical (the storage space is limited). Now, objects valued at less than 50 euros (90% of the stockpile) are saved for four months, and those having a higher value are kept for 18 months.

20. (a) Due to the proximity of the Citroën factory to the quai de Javel, the church (completed in 1930) is placed under the name of Saint Christopher, patron of voyagers by car, train, and plane, but also of skiers, cyclists, balloon and dirigible operators, sailors, climbers, train engineers and users of modern transportation! On the roof of the chancel, the saint is shown surrounded by voyagers begging his protection and touting the aforementioned means of locomotion: plane, balloon, train, steamship and automobile.

16TH ARRONDISSEMENT

✕

1. (b) The upper and lower lakes are linked by a waterfall.

2. (b) In 1987, for the centenary of the *International Herald Tribune*. Since August 1997, however, the replica of the torch of the Statue of Liberty has become a veritable mausoleum to the memory of Princess Diana, always piled with flowers and little notes written in numerous languages.

3. (a) Trocadéro was a fort situated near Cádiz (in Spain), which the French army liberated from insurgents threatening the Spanish throne in 1823, at the request of Ferdinand VII. A reproduction of the fort was erected in 1826 on the Chaillot hill, on the occasion of a military festival. Ever since, Trocadéro has rhymed with Chaillot (as per the added accent).

4. (b) The answer is in the question! Since the 1980s, the acrobatic spectacle of the champions of wheels from the club 340 — pronounced "Trois Quatre Zéro," a play on words recalling the "Trocadéro" — can be admired every Wednesday, Sunday and holiday.

5. (b) The Warsaw fountain shoots from 20 sidelong cannons, 56 sprayers and 12 water columns. The jets reach 50 m, 4 m and 7 m respectively.

6. (b) A happy coincidence...the Museum of Counterfeiting is installed in a late 19th-century town house that is an exact replica of an 18th-century residence in the Marais, which has since disappeared!

7. (c) Roland Garros was the first pilot to cross the Mediterranean by air, in 1913. He connected Fréjus to Bizerte (in Tunisia) in 7 hours and 53 minutes.

8. (a, b and c) All the answers are correct and complement each other. For 40,000 years the Albien water table has lain 700 m underground. As pure as the best mineral waters, it is rich in mineral salts and iron. It is said to do wonders for rheumatism.

9. (b) The Bacchic Brotherhood of Cupbearers of France set up its museum in an old limestone quarry. There is no Museum of Robots in Paris, and the Museum of Counterfeiting is housed on the rue de la Faisanderie.

10. (c) *The Electric Fairy*, painted by Raoul Dufy in 1937 for the electricity pavilion at the World's Fair, is an allegoric panorama 60 m wide by 10 m high. The paint is applied not to canvas, but to 250 plywood panels.

11. (b) The bois de Boulogne is the property of the city of Paris, as is the bois de Vincennes.

12. (b) "Friend of sound and enemy of noise," an expression attributed to Henry Bernard, the architect of the Maison de la Radio. The round shape of the building, opened in 1963, was dictated by the laws of acoustics, which call for the walls of a recording studio to be curved.

13. (b) The United States. Examples include the avenue du Président Kennedy, the avenue du Président Wilson, the avenue de New York, the place des États-Unis, the rue Benjamin Franklin and the statue of Washington.

14. (c) *The Fox and the Crow*. The statue of the great fable writer was sculpted in 1983 by Charles Correia.

15. (b) Jean-Baptiste Kléber, an Alsatian general, distinguished himself in the wars of the Revolution, notably in the Vendée, and participated in the Egyptian campaign at Napoleon's side.

16. (a) The name evokes an ancient tradition, consisting of hanging boxwood blessed as a cross, on Palm Sunday, to protect the health of a household and its children. In the 18th century there was a rue de la Croix-Boissière (Boxwood Cross Street) in this area.

17. (a) The museum has housed the exceptional collection of Émile Guimet, a rich industrialist from Lyon and enthusiast of Asian art, since 1889.

18. (c) A hunting pavilion frequented by Charles IX was erected on the site, where a pack of dogs was kept. The place was nicknamed "La Meute" ("The Pack") or, depending on the source used, "Les Mues" (the antlers of a fallen stag), which was transformed over the course of time into "La Muette."

19. (a) Léna is in Germany (in Thuringia).

20. (b) This African art museum, linked to the Dapper Foundation in Amsterdam, bears the name of a 17th century Dutch humanist. Dapper was a doctor and geographer, as well as the author of *A Description of Africa and its Islands* (1678), a pioneering work in its field, all without ever having left his birthplace of Holland!

17TH ARRONDISSEMENT

✖

1. (a) It was Bartholdi's mother, Augusta Charlotte, who served as his model.

2. (b) The station was christened "Obligado" in memory of the 1845 Franco-English victory in Argentina (which consisted of forcing passage through the gorge around an estuary of the río de la Plata).

3. (b) For the Pereires, banking was a family tradition. Émile and Isaac didn't stray; they financed the first French train lines and mounted large real estate operations (in the plaine Monceau quarter, but also in the southwest of France).

4. (a) These ancient villages and hamlets, like so many others, were annexed by the city of Paris in 1860.

5. (c) The "ratodrome" was a training school for dogs specializing in rat hunting, training them to pursue rodents, badgers and foxes to their burrows and to kill them. The attraction of the dog school was a system of betting and wagering, over drinks, on the chances that the dogs would kill a rat.

6. (b) The Notre-Dame-de-la-Compassion chapel was built on the site where prince Ferdinand d'Orléans (eldest son of Louis-Philippe) died on the 13th of July 1842, the victim of a traffic accident.

The chapel had to be moved a few dozen meters to permit the construction of the Boulevard Périphérique.

7. (b) Nana's town house was situated on the avenue de Villiers, on the corner of the rue Cardinet.

8. (a) At the end of the 19th century, Émile Gaillard, regent of the Banque de France, had a Renaissance-style palace built, inspired by the Blois and Gien chateaus (notably borrowing their brickwork, windows and chandeliers). After his death, the Banque de France acquired the building and opened a branch there in 1924.

9. (b) The first owners were required to plant three flowering trees in their gardens (access to the street is at 154 rue de Clichy and 59 rue de La Jonquière).

10. (b) The pilot Charles Godefroy — nicknamed the Black Baron — wanted to express the dissatisfaction of French aviators, who were bitter over having been made to march on foot (considered an affront) during the July 14th 1919 parade commemorating the signing of the Treaty of Versailles. He pulled off his exploit going 50 km/h in a Nieuport airplane. The fit of temper cost him the permanent revocation of his pilot's license.

11. (c) The "jeu de maillet" ("mail" meaning hammer) consisted of hitting a boxwood ball through a succession of iron arches with a mallet. "Mail" also came to mean the place where the game was practiced, on public squares and promenades.

12. (b) There are 12 avenues radiating from the square, giving rise to its old name "place de l'Étoile" ("Star Square").

13. (a) *La Marseillaise*. Rude asked his wife to serve as his model for the female character symbolizing victory. In order to capture the expression he was looking for, he exhorted her to "Shout! Shout louder!" while she was posing.

14. (b) Formerly called place de l'Étoile, it was re-christened place Charles-de-Gaulle in 1970, upon the death of the General. That said, neither Parisians nor tourists have managed to forget the more familiar usage, and everyone still calls it place de l'Étoile!

15. (a) Parmentier's plantations were surrounded by high fences and guarded, night and day, by armed men (who had orders to sleep with one eye open). As everything forbidden naturally attracts curiosity and coveting, the tubers were of course stolen, and avidly eaten.

16. (c) The rich collector was one of the first to light his salons with electricity...an innovation which women judged hardly flattering to their complexions.

17. (a) Dummies made of carved wood. The publication of the pieces played at the "Erotikon Theâtron" was banned by the law for insult against public morality and good values. A copy titled *Erotic Theatre of the rue de la Santé* is nevertheless kept in the national library's "Hell," its collection of pornographic materials.

18. (a) The bagotier ran behind taxis in order to help travelers carry their baggage once they arrived at their destination. These galloping porters were also called "pisteurs."

19. (b) The arrival of the elevator allowed a bourgeois clientele to effortlessly lift themselves to the higher floors, offering a wide panoramic view and less exposure to the nuisances of the road.

20. (a) The three terms designated communal transportation vehicles serving the principle towns around Paris. The location of the court at Versailles, notably, required incessant trips between the two towns. "Carabas" were carriages with multiple horses, while "coucous" and "chamber pots" were tiny cars pulled by a single horse, often packed to the point that travelers would make the trip on the roof!

18TH ARRONDISSEMENT

⚓

1. (b) The sculpture, the work of Jean Marais, pays homage to Marcel Aymé, the author of a novel that shared the sculpture's name. He lived not far from its location, on rue Norvins.

2. (a) The variety of white grape cultivated on the hill was designated "king of the vines" by a classification system implemented during the reign of Saint Louis.

3. (b) At the hour when the roller shutters come down, the rue Cavalotti takes on the appearance of an art gallery, as reproductions of famous canvases decorate the metallic shutters of its 20 shops.

4. (b) In refusing to remove his hat on the passage of the procession, the young chevalier de la Barre became a hero of secularists. His statue, which used to stand in front of Sacré-Coeur, was melted in 1941, and never replaced; all that remains is his empty pedestal.

5. (a) Since 1995, bluish optic fibers have drawn a "path of light" on the stairway-cum-road, reproducing the placement of the stars in the sky each year from January 1st to July 1st.

6. (a) Pushing 36 m below the surface, it holds the record for depth.

7. (c) The immaculate whiteness of the Basilica is due to the fact that it is built with stone from Château-Landon that, on contact with rain, secretes a white substance, calcite. The more it rains, the whiter it gets.

8. (c) The hefty Savoyarde (18,835 kg), offered by the Savoyard dioceses to the city of Paris, was cast at Annecy and installed at the summit of the Basilica in 1895.

9. (b) Since 1985, this little piece of restricted-access land has been protected from pruning shears, fertilizers, and weed-killers at the request of the residents of the neighborhood who solicitously watch over its flora and fauna, and who are given the vegetables raised there.

10. (a and c) Two Roman temples were situated at Montmartre, one dedicated to Mercury (the god of commerce and eloquence), the other to Mars (god of war). The presence of the latter would have given its name to the site (Mons Martis: The Mountain of Mars) had it not evoked Saint Denis (The Mountain of the Martyr).

11. (a) Although Boris Vian did live, for a time, at 6 cité Veron, it was Jacques Prévert, another habitant of the area, who was a child of the third (republic), and who lived on the fourth (floor) of a house from the nineteenth (century)... in the eighteenth (arrondissement).

12. (a) 1933. The first grape harvest festival was celebrated on October 3rd the next year. Since then, the tradition has continued; every first Saturday of October, the gardeners of the city of Paris harvest the Montmartre vineyard. The wine, aged in the cellars of the town hall of the 18th arrondissement, is tapped in mid-January. The 1,700 50-cl bottles produced are auctioned, the profits going to charitable works in the quarter.

13. (b) This Montmartois concert café was the site of the first Parisian strip tease. A young woman undressed there, leaving on only a skintight, flesh-colored garment.

14. (b) You should recognize in the name of the store a tribute (in slang) from the founder to his mother, who was named Tita.

15. (b) Only two windmills remain on Montmartre: le Radet (83 rue Lepic) and le Blute-Fin (75–77 rue Lepic).

16. (b) François Truffaut demanded that he be buried in the cimetière de Montmartre because he had been denied permission to shoot a sequence from *Love on the Run* there. It was a prohibition, however, of which the filmmaker barely took notice, shooting his scene clandestinely in the cemetery.

17. (c) The Lapin Agile, whose sign depicts a jolly hare dancing in a frying pan. It was drawn by the political caricaturist André Gill...from whom the name "Lapin à Gill" comes.

18. (b) The first review mounted by Jacki Clerico, *Frou-Frou*, was a success. Since then, out of superstition, the titles of all the reviews have begun with the letter F: *Frisson*, *Fascination*, *Festival*, *Follement*, *Frénésie*, *Femmes Femmes Femmes*, and *Formidable*. It's also a nod to the French cancan, which was born at the Moulin in 1889.

19. (b) Auguste Renoir is the creator of *Le Moulin de la Galette*.

20. (b) The Pepper Mill was, in 1865, the last windmill erected in Paris. It was located near the current 12 rue Junot.

19TH ARRONDISSEMENT

⚜

1. (c) This metro station possesses the longest escalator (20.32 m).

2. (b) The Sibyl's Temple, named after priestesses of Apollo and soothsayers.

3. (c) A croissant or, per your own imagination, a half moon, a rhinoceros horn, a bean, a drop of water...

4. (a) The Zénith de Paris is located on the edge of the parc de La Villette, between the canal de l'Ourcq and the Boulevard Périphérique. A few years ago, a plane hoisted to the top of the old feed lift of the La Villette slaughterhouses signaled the Zénith from afar. The tower no longer exists, but the plane remains, since attached to the top of a Bernard Tschumi folly, which houses the ticket booth.

5. (b) The pont de Crimée, recognizable by its four great metallic pulleys, is the last hydraulic lift bridge in Paris. The pont de la Grange-aux-Bells and the pont de la rue Dieu (on the canal Saint-Martin, in the 10th arrondissement) are swing bridges.

6. (b) The appearance of Halley's Comet (which is visible every 76 years). During the opening night of the Cité des sciences, the two thousand guests were thrust into the thick of modern technology thanks to images collected by a probe and projected on a giant screen. It was also the day when the Mir space station welcomed its first visitors: two Soviet cosmonauts who moved into the orbiting station.

7. (c) Volgograd. While the Parisian square (referring to the battle) kept the city's old name, the rue de Saint-Pétersbourg (in the 8th) has changed its name several times, in sync with the Russian city: it has been successively called de Saint-Pétersbourg, then de Petrograd (1917-1945), de Leningrad (1945-1991) and de Saint-Pétersbourg again (since 1991).

8. (b) Professor Robert Debré (1882–1978) was department head at the Hospital for Sick Children from 1940 to 1957; he contributed to the progress of pediatrics and the protection of childhood health.

9. (b) This Jean Dubuffet sculpture is officially called *The Welcoming*, but the young patients hospitalized at Robert-Debré call it "The Clown."

10. (a) They can't be too heavy, as they're situated above old quarries. Built on sloping land, they give the impression of clinging to each other so as not to slip.

11. (c) The painter felt attracted to, even mesmerized by the gare Saint-Lazare. Ironically, several of the canvases he painted of it are today displayed in the old gare d'Orsay, which has been transformed into a museum. The Claude Monet Villa, in the 19th arrondissement, is on one of the private streets in the Mouzaïa quarter.

12. (b) The Seine has its source at an altitude of 471 m on the Langres Plateau, near Dijon, and runs a total of 776 km to the English Channel. Paradoxically, the quai de la Seine (in the 19th) is nowhere near the Seine!

13. (b) They were called Mississippi Quarries because the gypsum extracted there was to be exported to the new world. The image of Mississippi might also have been evoked simply because the sites were far from the center of the city.

14. (c) The total length of the Périphérique is 35.04 km.

15. (c) Employed by cabaret owners and other wine sellers, the "guardian angels" took charge of their clients at the exit of the bar and assured their safety until they arrived home. They sometimes had to help them face the wrath of their wives, guide them to their beds or even tuck them in! A candidate to become a guardian angel had to pass a very serious exam aiming to evaluate three essential qualities: unfailing sobriety, great physical strength and a subtle sense of customer relations.

16. (b) The octroi, a highly unpopular tax, represented 60% of the city's takings. The financial wall endured until the relatively recent date of 1943. The Wall of the Farmers-General was broken by 60 gateways, of which only four remain: the portes de La Villette (Stalingrad), du Trône (place de la Nation), d'Enfer (Denfert-Rochereau), and de Chartres (parc Monceau).

17. (a) The tickets read "Upon exiting, throw in garbage."

18. (a) The term "banlieu" goes back to the 15th century and the extension of the city. It designated an area within a 4.5-km radius of the capital, over which the city's right of command and justice system stretched.

19. (b) A "cayenne" is a house that welcomes "compagnons du Tour de France." The one in the 19th arrondissement houses a small museum where models made by carpentry apprentices are kept.

20. (b) The La Villette site was the seat of Parisian slaughterhouses from the Second Empire until 1974, the date after which animals were no longer slaughtered within the city limits. The building set aside for the slaughterhouses became, after a transformation, the Cité des sciences et de l'industrie.

20TH ARRONDISSEMENT

⋙

1. (b) This U-shaped road has the peculiarity of having two consecutive intersections with another road (the rue de Bagnolet). You think you're retracing your own steps when in fact it's the road that's made the half circle!

2. (c) The road isn't short on spirituality, as it is home to three different places of worship. One can find the Notre-Dame-de-la-Croix Church at number 2, an Ashkenazi synagogue at number 75, and the Reform Church of Belleville at number 97. As for the name Julien Lacroix, it was simply that of an old landowner.

3. (c) The first telegraph message, sent from Saint-Martin-du-Tertre (in what is today the Val-d'Oise) was received at 40 rue du Télégraphe (the highest point in Paris, at 148 m). The transmission took place thanks to mechanical relays placed on high points, spaced approximately 10 km apart. After being observed with a telescope, the signals were retransmitted to the next relay.

4. (c) Raymond Roussel, a writer who died in 1933, practiced experimental writing (the Surrealists would later claim his work) and was a chess master. He demanded to be buried in a 32-square vault (in the cemetery's 89th division).

5. (c) The Parisian bourgeois shunned the newly created cemetery. In order to promote it, the prefect Frochot had the idea of transferring the remains (albeit of dubious authenticity) of a few illustrious personalities. The prestige-seeking operation succeeded far beyond what had been hoped for. The people of Paris — flattered by the idea of *post-mortem* mingling with celebrities — were banging at the gates, and the tombs were snatched up like hotcakes.

6. (a) He even went so far as to specify:

> "My dear friends, when I die,
> Plant a willow in the cemetery.
> I like its tearful foliage;
> To me its pallor is sweet and dear,
> And its shadow will be light
> On the ground where I will rest."

Since then, the willow shading Musset's tomb has been regularly changed, as the earth of the plot is not very hospitable for the species.

7. (c) The Père-Lachaise Cemetery is housed on the rue du Repos, two steps from the rue des Couronnes. The rue de Paradis and the passage d'Enfer exist, but in other arrondissements (the 10th and the 14th, respectively).

8. (a) The escalator, invented in the United States, was presented to France during the World's Fair of 1900, and installed nine years later in the Père-Lachaise metro station.

9. (a) *Old Goriot*. With these words, the ambitious Rastignac issues a challenge to the capital and its pitiless jungle.

10. (a) They smashed the scandalously prominent part with blows from rocks. The turmoil surrounding the tomb of Oscar Wilde (in the 89th cemetery division) has never let up. In the year 2000, it was covered in red kisses. The romantic splattering wasn't to the liking of the executor of the plot who, sick of cleaning fees, had protective glass installed over the granite.

11. (a) Touching the statue of Victor Noir augmented the fertility of women and helped young ladies procure a husband. This power is associated with the highly flattering phallic protuberance of the reclining statue in the question. The appendage shines with a peculiar luster, having been polished by the caresses of thousands of women needing a husband or a child.

12. (a) The Belleville Apaches were so nicknamed, in 1902, because of their cruelty, which made that of the Indians they were named after look docile. Their leader fought the leader of the rival Popincouty gang for the favor of Amélie Hélie, nicknamed "Golden Helmet."

13. (a) It was an *Elephas primigenius*, similar to the Siberian mammoth.

14. (b) The habitants of Ménilmontant are called Ménilmontants.

15. (b) The road was constructed in 1812, on the site of a vineyard called "Pas Noyaux" ("No Pits") because its grapes had no pits.

16. (a) The dog watcher offered a "light meal" (fresh water and a few bits of sugar) to his/her half-hour charges, who quietly waited for their master at the gates of the cemetery. One could also find a basket watcher and bag watcher at the gates of cemeteries.

17. (c) The rue Gasnier-Guy presents a 17.4% gradient.

18. (a) Stanislas Lépine and Albert Marquet (who gave his name to a road in the 20th arrondissement) were both captivated by the quays and bridges of the Seine, which they made recurring themes in their canvases. Boulevards at nightfall were more the specialty of Édouard Cortès.

19. (c) Beijing's giant through road is called Zhongzhou Road. Of a size comparable to that of Paris's, it was formed, like Paris's, over several centuries. The passage de Pékin, in the 20th arrondissement, is much more modest!

20. (b) The Museum of Air is an interactive museum totally dedicated to the element.